MAKING WORDS WORK

A PRACTICAL GUIDE TO WRITING POWERFUL CONTENT

KIM SCARAVELLI

Tellwell Talent
www.tellwell.ca

ISBN
978-0-2288-7007-4 (Paperback)
978-0-2288-7008-1 (eBook)

TABLE OF CONTENTS

To my daughters.

Love you to the moon and back.

You inspire me.

INTRODUCTION

My father was a mechanic by trade *and* by inclination.

On weekdays, he worked a union job, repairing giant trucks and snowplows. On weekends, he puttered in the garage, fixing old cars for neighbourhood teens and happily tinkering with everything from lawnmowers to vacuum cleaners.

He was a great mechanic and a lovely dad.

Over the years, I spent a fair bit of time watching my father work. I learned nothing about vehicle maintenance. *Embarrassing truth: I still struggle to top up the windshield wiper fluid.*

But I did figure out what it takes to truly excel at something, and it boils down to three basic principles:

1. **Honour the work.** Create a pleasant, productive workspace where things are organized properly and you feel comfortable. Make it as easy as possible to settle in and do your thing.

   Dad's garage was uber-functional. There was a place for every tool and a tool for every place. But he also had a stereo with decent speakers, and a little snack corner with store-bought cookies, an electric kettle, and a giant jar of Red Rose teabags. He understood the value of both utility and comfort.

2. **Take pride in your skills.** Appreciate the value you bring to the world, and constantly seek opportunities to practise and improve.

   Despite ongoing accolades from co-workers, who considered him a mechanical genius, dad never rested on his laurels. He was always going to car shows, reading automotive magazines, and poking around in junkyards looking for something he could creatively repurpose. My dad got a genuine kick out of learning new things.

3. **Truly enjoy what you do.** Take pleasure in the process, not just the product.

   Dad didn't pay much attention to the clock. By his way of thinking, work was finished when it was finished. Folks praised his diligence and patience, but I knew the truth. Dad simply lost track of time when he was merrily solving some mechanical dilemma.

Instead of a garage, I have a tiny-home office in my backyard. And I work with words, which are considerably less messy than engine parts. But my father's approach to things holds true, even in a digital world that didn't exist in his lifetime. His core belief was that anything worth doing was worth doing well.

In this book, I'm going to show you how to get into the right mindset for writing. I'll open my writer's toolbox and show you how to build powerful sentences and paragraphs. I'll share tips and tricks to help you attract and engage readers and create content that educates, entertains, and inspires.

Ultimately, I will do my best to help you feel excited about writing, because that's the real trick of the trade!

Thank you for buying my book. It is my pleasure to be part of your journey as a content writer.

WHO IS THIS BOOK FOR?

This book is for anyone who writes purposeful things online. Check out the following list. If you see yourself in one of the descriptions, you've come to the right place.

This book is for:

- **Copywriters and content writers** who want practical advice from someone who's been in the trenches for a long time. You'll learn how to up your game, polish your work, and avoid occupational hazards, like writer's block and burnout.

- **Business owners who write content for themselves** and want to do it well. You'll learn the basics of writing online and how to build brand authority using words.

- **Folks who have personal projects on the go**, like blogs or books, and want to develop a strong voice, tell stories well, and build a community of readers. You'll learn how to match your tone and style to online formats, and how to get more eyeballs on your content.

- **Business leaders who pay others for words** and want to learn what high-quality, effective content looks like. You'll learn what elevates powerful writing from space filler. This makes it easier to tell people what you want and judge the value of what you get.

BEFORE YOU GET STARTED

**"The talking about the thing isn't the thing.
Doing the thing is the thing."**

Amy Poehler, Actor, Comedian, and Author

Reading about writing makes you a reader. Taking classes about writing makes you a student. Simply pondering the art of writing makes you a ponderer. And it's super-cool to be well-read, well-versed, and well-aware of your inner thoughts.

But at some point, you just need to **do the thing.**

I'm happy that you bought my book, but I'll be disappointed if you spend countless hours scrolling through my words of wisdom instead of writing, because **writers write.**

To become a great writer, you must hone your craft through continuous practice. So right now, before you settle in with a cup of tea or a glass of wine, get up and find a notebook. *And not the Notes app on your phone.*

I want you to go old school, with paper and pen. Trust me on this. There's something uniquely satisfying about filling a notebook with ideas. Plus, as an added benefit, the complicated brain processes involved in manually writing on paper helps you remember things.

Keep your notebook open while you're reading. Jot down points you want to remember, and if something sparks an idea, get that pen moving right away. Elaborate on your thoughts. Do everything you can to fan that spark into a fire.

Note: If a fire ignites, I recommend that you shift to a keyboard and begin actually writing something. Notebooks are for ideas, not content assembly. The online world is where your words will live, so that's where you should plant them.

PART 1
Set the Stage for Success

Your work as a writer takes place in two spaces: the physical location where you pluck away on a keyboard, and that nebulous region of your brain where you turn thoughts into words. To write productively, you need both spaces to be well organized and welcoming.

Your physical surroundings are usually easy to renovate because you can see the challenges and you can buy solutions. *Never underestimate the motivational value of an ergonomic chair and a scented soy candle.*

The space between your ears may present bigger challenges, but it also reaps bigger rewards. Because once your mindset is in good shape and your imagination is firing on all cylinders, you can do *anything*!

In this section, I'm going to talk about ways to strengthen your creativity by cultivating comfort in both your physical and emotional environments. *If you're itching to skip this mumbo jumbo and jump forward to the sections about writing and editing, I encourage you to take a breath.* That itchiness is a problem. It's pulling you forward too fast and making it harder to learn new things.

In the short term, prioritizing speed over everything else may work out for you. But over the long haul, it increases your risk of burnout, which ultimately leads to lower quality work and unhappiness.

Give yourself permission to stop skimming.

CHAPTER 1
Develop Your Creativity Muscles

Myth: Creativity is a gift from the Gods. Some folks have it; others don't.

Reality: ALL humans area creative. Creativity is one of the special things that separates us from the other creatures wandering the planet. It's an integral part of our humanity.

It saddens me to hear someone say they're "just not creative". It breaks my heart because it's such an unnecessary limitation.

If you've been made to doubt your creativity, let me start by reassuring you. You are a beautiful, creative being. *Whoever planted that malignant thought in your childhood brain is a poopy-head and you can tell them I said so.*

I'm creative, you're creative, and everyone you bump into on the sidewalk is creative. Period.

We all begin flexing our creativity muscles at a young age. Some folks are more inclined—or more encouraged—to keep flexing. Their muscles strengthen, and they become more confident about their creative powers.

Confidence inspires action, so those kids continue to paint and draw, sing and dance, and write. And the more they create, the more capable of creating they become. That's it. That's how creativity works.

It isn't a gift from the Gods. **Creativity is a gift we give ourselves.**

Think of it this way: If you want stronger legs, you walk more. If you want stronger arms, you lift things. So, if you want stronger creativity, you need to flex those mental muscles in challenging ways.

I know you bought this book to improve your content writing skills. You may not be interested in painting and drawing or singing and dancing, but here's the thing—your creativity muscles are all connected.

When you let loose and dance around the kitchen, it's not just your dance moves that improve. And when you splash a bunch of paint on a canvas, you get more out of the experience than wall art. Engaging in other forms of creative expression ultimately strengthen your writing skills.

Is my artwork as solid as my writing? Definitely not! But I love the process of creating something bold and colourful, and I swear my writing's better after I've been painting.

I'm deliberate about exercising my creativity and you should be too. Here are a few tips to help strengthen your creativity muscles into a six-pack:

- **Set aside time each day to let your mind wander.** Start small. You'll be surprised how far your thoughts can travel in as little as 10 minutes. Pick a random subject to start you off but let your thoughts fly free. Don't take notes, or poke around online, or *do* anything at all. Just think.

This may feel uncomfortable at first. We live in a world that associates productivity and value with *doing* things but thinking should always come before doing! Training yourself to think deeply will help you as a writer—and as a human.

- **Keep a notebook with you. Always.** When you let your mind go exploring regularly, new ideas appear more often. Some may help with content writing, some may not. But every interesting idea deserves to be acknowledged, so write them all down.

- **Try new ways of expressing yourself with words.** Create poetry. Write songs. Challenge yourself to craft a short story. Venture outside your comfort zone because that's where all the best things happen.

- **Share your creativity with the world.** Creativity thrives on connection, and the more you share your work with others, the less self-conscious you become about doing so. Putting yourself out there builds confidence.

As long as you're having fun, keep pushing yourself. Set aside longer, more frequent amounts of time for just thinking. Fill shelves with beautiful notebooks full of your ideas. Collaborate with other creative folks whenever there's a chance to do so. Be boldly, unapologetically creative!

To quote the always brilliant Maya Angelou: **"You can't use up creativity. The more you use, the more you have."**

CHAPTER 2
Read. Read. Read.

Have you ever enjoyed a delicious meal at a restaurant and then been inspired to try making it at home? Or maybe you've seen an outfit on someone else and then bought something similar?

We get ideas from others all the time. It's a natural part of how people learn. We observe. We find things that pique our interest. Then we experiment and put our own spin on those things.

If you want to stretch your creativity and improve your writing skills, you should expose yourself to as much written text as possible. Because the more you read, the more things you discover about language and how to use it. **Reading is how you come to appreciate and understand the art and the science of writing.**

That said, don't stress out about how much time you spend at it. Reading is supposed to be a joy, not a chore. On some days, a few online articles may be all you've got the time or mental bandwidth for. Don't sweat it.

Variety is the spice of life. Blogs. Magazines. Even technical stuff, like white papers and reports. It's all fodder for your imagination. A few books should always be in play because they're substantial, but that doesn't mean you have to pour yourself into them daily.

Secret truth: I have at least three books on the go at any given time, usually a mix of fiction and non-fiction titles. Sometimes I finish them, sometimes I don't, and that's okay.

Because *every* page is filled with words, ideas, and inspiration. And if I get distracted and wander off to read something else, the remaining pages wait for me. *Books are very amicable!*

If you've temporarily lost the habit of reading, as busy folks sometimes do, here are a few tips and tricks to help you get back on track:

- **Start with an easy time commitment, say 20 minutes a day.** This is enough to feel like you're achieving something, but not so long that it scrambles the rest of your day.

- **Highlight phrases and passages that resonate with you.** Interacting with the words makes the experience more dynamic and helps you stay focused. This is especially important when you're a bit out of practice at reading and easily distracted.

- **Read hard copy books with paper pages.** In today's world of screens, there's something decadent about curling up with a book. *It feels like a treat—and who doesn't like treats?*

Over time, reading more will help you write more, and write better. It's not quite like osmosis. You won't absorb great writing skills just by touching the beautiful words of others, but you will start to notice what appeals to you. And you'll feel challenged to experiment and play with words, which is why it's so important to read. And read more. And keep reading.

CHAPTER 3
Befriend the Notebook

"Write down the thoughts of the moment. Those that come unsought for are commonly the most valuable."

Francis Bacon, Author, Philosopher, and Politician

I keep notebooks everywhere:

- Beside my bed

- On my coffee table

- In my kitchen junk drawer

- In beach bags, handbags, and knapsacks

- In my glove compartment

- In a glass cabinet in my office

- Stashed under a stack of towels in my bathroom (*Don't judge me. I get great ideas in the shower, in the tub, and yes, on the toilet.*)

The short-term memory can only cling to information for about three minutes, and that's on a good day when you're not stressed, over-worked, or otherwise distracted. That means you've got 180 seconds to find a home for the brilliant thought that burst spontaneously into your mind. After that, it's gone forever.

Sure, you could send yourself a text or an email or throw a few words into the Notes app on your phone. *I do all that stuff, but I find notebooks more satisfying.*

There's something about the physical act of putting pen to paper that confirms your identity as a writer. **You make things with words!**

Even when your notebooks are closed, just having them around asserts that you're creative. And when you settle a newborn thought on the unfettered space of an empty page, it doesn't just sit there. It moves. Expands. Stretches in all sorts of directions.

Your notebooks keep you from forgetting things—and that's great. But what they really do is set your ideas free. That's what makes them magical!

CHAPTER 4
Create a Productive Writing Space

In my fantasy life, I write from a balcony on the top floor of a charming apartment in Sorrento, Italy. There's a fresh latte to the left of my keyboard, I hear music from buskers working on the street below, and everything smells like lemons.

FYI: I have sat on that balcony with the fresh latte and the smell of lemons, and it was glorious. Until I opened my laptop and discovered that the Wi-Fi connection was spotty, the table wobbled, and the buskers were kind of distracting. Also, one fellow had a truly unfortunate singing voice.

Where you write is important because you should feel comfortable and relaxed. But you also need to factor in the practical realities of the writing process.

Wants: Exotic locations that provide serenity, solitude, and spiritual inspiration.

Needs: An accessible electrical outlet, a sturdy table, reliable internet service, and a decent chair. *Because poor ergonomics are a workplace hazard.*

The problem with placing too much value on where you write and what kind of vibe you create is that these obsessions tend to become excuses for not writing.

On the flip side, I know a few folks who have tried to consistently create content in busy kitchens, cramped bedrooms, and crowded coffee shops. And none of them have happy memories about those experiences.

I've been writing for decades, in cubicles and offices, and in various parts of my home. And here's what I've learned about creating a productive workspace:

- **Stake your claim.** Your work deserves respect, and you demonstrate that respect by establishing a designated space to do your thing. Even if it's a very tiny table in the corner of a very tiny room, it should be yours, and yours alone. *If you've got roommates or family, train them not to use this space.*

- **Add things that bring you joy.** Have you got a mug that holds just the right amount of coffee? A favourite book or two? A piece of wall art that makes you smile? Even if your writing space is small, I'm sure you can squeeze in at least a few joy-inducing items.

- **Expand over time.** As you write more (*and you will*), and as you take greater ownership of your title as a writer (*which will also happen*), reward yourself with a bit more space and a few more joyful items. Spread out. Claim more territory. Make you—the writer—increasingly visible.

Location isn't everything, but it's something. And you deserve to enjoy where you work.

CHAPTER 5
Minimize Clutter and Distraction

Clutter is defined as "scattered or disordered things that impede movement or reduce effectiveness."[1]

Scattered. Disordered. Impeded. Reduced. These are <u>not</u> words you want associated with your work life.

I have two desk drawers filled with useful things, like highlighters, paper clips, and a significant collection of lip balms. When I want them, I know where to find them. But I don't leave everything scattered about because messiness is a distraction.

As a content writer, you commonly collect many things before you start a first draft, like:

- Information you've unearthed about your topic

- Research into your ideal audience, keywords, and direction.

- Client input if that's a factor

---

[1] "Clutter." *Merriam-Webster.com Dictionary*, Merriam-Webster, https://www.merriam-webster.com/dictionary/clutter.

- Fun facts, quotes, and statistics

- Photos and illustrations

These are all useful. In fact, I mention them in several chapters. But they don't need to be in front of your nose all the time.

Before you start that first draft, look through everything. Make notes if you need to, save your documents and images in a folder, bookmark relevant links, then close everything. Open files and programs only as you need them and close them when their purpose has been served.

And don't succumb to the temptation of leaving unrelated tabs open! Shut down news sites, social media platforms, games, personal apps, and email. It's easier to stay on task when there isn't non-essential foolishness begging for your attention.

Leaving tabs open is indicative of a bad habit known as "task switching". You think you're multi-tasking and staying on top of everything, but in reality you're diluting your focus and interrupting your creativity.

While working, both your physical and virtual desktops should remain tidy. Clear your space *and* your mind. Minimize clutter and distraction.

CHAPTER 6
Don't Wait for Inspiration

**"Amateurs sit and wait for inspiration,
the rest of us just get up and go to work."**

Stephen King, Author

If you're writing for fun, feel free to wait for that magical moment when the muse sits on your shoulder and whispers sweetly in your ear. But if getting words onto the page is part of how you earn a living, inspiration can't be a mandatory pre-requisite. In fact, waiting to feel motivated is a terrible idea because *no one* can conjure up inspiration whenever they need it.

Feelings fluctuate, so if you want to consistently create content, you've got to move away from the motivation model. The alternative isn't sexy, but it gets results...

Just get up and go to work.

Commit to a certain amount of time each day. Schedule it on your calendar, just like you schedule other stuff. Then show up and get it done, whether you feel like it or not.

I apologize if I'm making the creative process sound like one more chore on your to-do list. That's truly not my intention. But you bought this book because you want to elevate your writing and meet your content creation goals. Self-discipline is going to help you get there; waiting for motivation isn't.

That said, there's no need to suffer. I'm writing this chapter from my very cozy office space. There's a lavender-scented soy candle burning. I've got a fresh mug of peppermint tea on my desk. It's lovely.

But I've also got the timer on my phone set to one hour. While that timer's ticking away, I'm not sneaking peeks at social media, checking email, or answering my phone. And I'm *definitely not* waiting to feel inspired. This is my content creation time so I'm hunkering down and clicking away on the keyboard for 60 minutes. No excuses.

Some days, I accomplish great things. Other days, I do not. But I always manage to pull something out of my head and shape it into words, and it's surprising how often inspiration comes to me only *after* I've started that timer!

CHAPTER 7
Embrace Self-Imposed Deadlines

**"A deadline is negative inspiration.
Still, it's better than no inspiration at all."**

Rita Mae Brown, Author and Screenwriter

Writing is a solitary task. It's just you and the keyboard. You may have deadlines for delivering completed content to an employer, a client, or yourself. But chances are that no one's looming over your shoulder, keeping you on task. Ultimately, you are 100% responsible for your progress so you need to **be your own task master**.

When it comes to writing, self-imposed deadlines establish a concrete ending to a process that might otherwise go on forever. There's always some little addition, or deletion, or twisting of a phrase, that could make a piece of writing marginally better. *I could edit and adjust forever!*

Self-imposed deadlines are a must because they maintain both productivity and sanity. Once I set a deadline, I can see the finish line. If something must be completed by end of the day on Friday, then that's what "done" looks like. It's a solid point in time and space.

The big secret to making self-imposed deadlines work is to take them seriously. Treat them with the same degree of respect you would give a deadline set by an employer or client.

The other secret is to reward yourself. I'm a huge fan of self-bribery. My favourite treats include:

- Trips to a bookstore (*my sacred place*)

- Self-care activities, like manicures

- Foods (*especially the kind you get in bakeries*)

Don't make excuses. Just get 'er done. *Then treat yourself because you're worth it!*

CHAPTER 8
Be Proactive About Avoiding Writer's Burnout

The internet is a voracious content beast. Even if you write all day, every day, for weeks on end, it will still be hungry for more. And the critical voice in your head can be insistent and unreasonable, always driving you to jump higher and run faster.

When insatiable demand meets limitless expectation, you're at risk of burnout.

The good news is that writer's burnout doesn't happen overnight. It's the cumulative result of stressing and over-working for too long. Think of it as a repetitive strain injury that can be avoided through preventive care.

As someone who relies on creating content to pay the mortgage and keep the refrigerator stocked, I've learned firsthand that working at a sustainable pace is critical. Mini holidays can't save you, so long as you're secretly obsessing about all the stuff you need to do when you get back to work.

I'm not going to get into the details of how I manage my workload or client expectations, because what works for me may not work for you. My sustainable pace may be faster or slower than yours, and my degree of professional autonomy may be greater or less than yours.

That said, there's one commonality all content writers share: we have stuff to write. And I speak from experience when I say that time management, success, and peace of mind all come easier when you define each bit of "stuff" in clear, do-able terms.

Vague goals can leave you working to the brink of exhaustion, while seldom enjoying a sense of accomplishment. To reduce the risk of burnout, you need to transition blurry ambitions into specific, measurable, achievable deliverables.

Blurry ambitions:

- Write some blog posts

- Make website content better

- Learn more about search engine optimization

How many is "some"? What does "better" look like? How much "more" do you need to learn? Imagine these as items on a to-do list. How would you know when they were done to your satisfaction?

Specific, measurable, achievable deliverables:

- Write two blog posts, 1,000-1,500 words each.

- Update a website page to include you-and-I language, three testimonials, and a call to action.

- Spend one hour on authority websites, learning about a particular topic. Bookmark each website for future reference.

With deliverables like these, it's easy to track your progress, pace yourself, and feel triumph when you cross the finish line. Then, like any other elite athlete, you can transition into cool-down time and enjoy some hard-earned rest.

Burnout is an occupational hazard for content writers, so do whatever you can to set a sustainable pace. Try to challenge yourself without pushing too hard, for too long.

Most of all, listen to your body. Don't ignore warning signs, like sleep problems, anxiety, or an increased lack of enthusiasm for work you used to enjoy. Take these things seriously and seek help promptly.

Always prioritize your mental and physical health over deadlines and ambitions.

PART 2
Collect Your Thoughts

Imagine yourself on a stage. Your only instruction is to speak for 15 minutes on the subject of "business". You have no details about the event, the attendees, or what aspect of business they want to hear about.

The odds of delivering an impactful, polished, and professional speech under such conditions are practically zero.

Effective communication, whether verbal or in writing, must start with a solid grasp of *what* you're communicating about and *why it matters*. The more clearly you understand these things, the easier it becomes to find the right words and use them with precision and power.

It can be tempting to skip the research and preparation work, especially when you're busy and a deadline is looming. The voice in your head may start insisting that you know enough already. But don't listen - that voice is leading you astray!

Flailing forward seldom ends well, in writing or in life.

In this section, I'm going to talk about how to identify your primary purpose, research your topic, and organize your thoughts, *before* you start writing.

CHAPTER 9
Know Your Primary Purpose

Content that serves a clear purpose is more apt to thrive online. Every piece of writing doesn't need to be Biblically profound, but it should provide value to readers. Otherwise, it's just word pollution.

As a writer, you will also find it easier and more rewarding to create words of value. Stronger writing naturally flows from a stronger sense of purpose.

Purpose impacts every element of content from topic to tone, so you should clearly understand your *why* before you start putting words on the page. In general, your primary purpose will fall into one of these categories:

- **Informing or educating.** People have questions, concerns, and knowledge gaps. They want to know more about events, trends, and topics. Informational content usually provides an overview of a subject and answers general questions, while educational content goes deeper, offers instruction, and tends to use more formal language and tone. Both serve to demonstrate expertise and build authority.

Examples: how-to articles, checklists, reviews, case studies, white papers, e-books, e-learning modules.

- **Entertaining.** People are attracted to heart-warming content that makes them smile, so this type of writing usually involves upbeat topics and a friendly tone. It can still be impactful. Entertaining content is highly shareable and a great way to establish rapport, humanize brands, and build trust. It's important stuff!

  Examples: humorous stories, personal narratives, quizzes, posts filled with fun facts.

- **Inspiring readers to do something.** You may be inspiring readers to do anything from making a purchase to donating to a cause, kickstarting a lifestyle change, or joining a social movement. Inspirational content is designed to motivate action, so it tends to use strong, dynamic words and descriptions.

  Examples: promotional writing (aka copywriting), lifestyle pieces, website landing pages.

You can hit more than one target with a single piece of writing. But first and foremost, your words should honour their primary purpose. This book is a good example.

Not to toot my own horn, but I'm a funny person, and I've tried to make this an entertaining read. That said, my first draft had a heavier dose of humour than the version you're reading now.

During the editing process, I ruthlessly murdered dozens of witty asides. Yes, they would have made you smile, but they were also somewhat off-topic and potentially distracting.

This is not a book of amusing narratives with a bit of writing advice. It's a book of writing advice with a light-hearted tone. I hope you're entertained—because learning happens easier when you're not bored to death. But ultimately, I want you to remember this book as informative and helpful.

CHAPTER 10
Respect the Difference Between Copywriting and Content Writing

"Nobody reads ads. People read what interests them. Sometimes it's an ad."

Howard Gossage, Advertising Executive from the 1950s

The terms "copywriting" and "content writing" get churned together so often that it becomes easy to believe they're synonyms, but they're not. **All copywriting is content writing but not all content writing is copywriting.**

Clear as mud?

Copywriting is umbilically connected to sales and has existed for as long as folks have been selling products and services. The purpose of all copywriting is to inspire action and that action is directly related to purchasing something.

If you're creating website landing pages, product pages, or online promotions, you're writing copy. As such, your focus should be on selecting powerful words that deliver a big emotional punch, because emotion drives action. And you want to be as succinct as possible because too many words can water down your message and reduce your impact. Clear, concise writing is always desirable, but it's particularly important in copywriting.

Content writing is a broader concept that may or may not be related to marketing. For example, there are blogs that exist purely to entertain or educate. But the majority, including many that are entertaining and educational, are also part of a marketing strategy. Their long-term purpose is to build brand authority and drive more traffic to a website. The posts themselves aren't ads, but they may include links to sales-related pages.

Content writing frequently involves creating longer pieces, which many view—rightly or wrongly—as more valuable demonstrations of expertise. Examples include online articles and blog posts, case studies, white papers, and e-books. Having said that, content writing can also involve shorter formats, like social media posts.

Whether you're creating copy or content, the basic requirements are the same. To write something worthwhile, you need:

- A deep understanding of your reader and what they're looking for

- Enough knowledge of your subject to provide value

- Creativity and skills as a wordsmith

One type of writing is not necessarily better or more worthy than the other, they simply serve different purposes. That said, it's important to be 100% transparent with readers, so don't disguise ad copy as informational or educational content. This is both a professional and ethical no-no. *And there's nothing people hate worse than the feeling that they've been duped into reading a sales pitch!*

CHAPTER 11
Focus on Substance and Value

"Don't settle for style. Succeed in substance."

Wynton Marsalis, Jazz Musician

In the world of writing, there's a common misconception that length and substance are somehow intertwined. In truth, you can create 500 words of complete brilliance. Conversely, you can assemble 5,000 words of meaningless drivel.

Longer pieces give you more room to explore a topic. But you cannot create greater value, authority, or credibility, by simply putting more words into the mix, because **substance is about depth, not length**.

Substantial content happens when you give readers meaningful, high-quality information and insights that match or exceed their expectations. To transition from superficial to substantial, you need to:

- Add solid facts to back up insights and opinions.

- Provide practical guidance rather than just talk *about* a subject.

- Use a style and tone that matches your purpose and makes your words easy to read and digest.

Facts come in many forms, including:

- Statistics, studies, and research findings from reputable sources
- Quotes from well-known experts
- Reviews and testimonials from real-life people

Likewise, practical guidance can be presented in several ways. For instance, you can:

- Break complex concepts and processes into step-by-step instructions.
- Use personal stories to add context (e.g., describe a mistake you made and explain how to avoid it).
- Add examples or case studies to illustrate key points.
- Insert visual elements, like photos, illustrations, and graphs, to aid comprehension.

Tone and style are more nuanced. Ultimately, you want to play with your words until the presentation aligns with the purpose. For example, if your primary purpose is to educate, readers might expect a bit more formal language and a deeper dive into the topic than if your primary purpose is to entertain.

Remember that substance is about communicating something of value to your readers. **It's about quality rather than quantity.**

CHAPTER 12
Research Your Topic

**"No clever arrangement of bad eggs
ever made a good omelette."**

C.S. Lewis, Writer and Theologian

When you don't know enough about your topic to effectively write about it, research is a must. But even if you're an authority on a subject, there's value in finding facts and data to support your insights.

Good news: The internet has tons of information on any topic.

Bad news: The internet has *tons* of information on any topic.

So, the question is how do you find the *good* eggs? And avoid the *bad* ones?

When researching, your goal is to find accurate, timely, and objective information from reputable sources. Beyond that, you're looking for particularly interesting tidbits that reflect a deep knowledge or unique perspective.

Common sources of reliable information may include:

- Transcripts of interviews and public speeches

- Statistical data (e.g., census reports)

- Surveys from reputable companies and organizations

- Journal articles and reviews

- Academic sources (e.g., research books, research papers)

- Government agencies and official organizations

On the flip side, here are a few *less* reliable sources:

- **Websites that rely on sponsored and/or contributed content** may not be fact-checking diligently. Just because a fact made its way onto one of those websites, that doesn't make it true.

- **Personal blogs** may be written by credible authorities who are reliable sources of information. But in general, personal blogs tend to be highly opinionated, and many dress up fiction as fact. Approach with caution.

- **Social media** is a wild and crazy space. The speed with which a social media platform can amplify and lend credence to a falsehood is terrifying. Any fact that comes to you via social media should be investigated thoroughly and dissected under a microscope!

Taking the time to research your topic is always worth the effort. When you use reliable sources, validate your facts, and properly cite references, you demonstrate a level of professionalism that immediately elevates your writing.

Good research is one of the foundational elements of high-quality content.

CHAPTER 13
Pick Your Keywords and Use Them Well

I won't lie to you. Getting found online is hard, and there's no magic formula that will catapult your content to page one of the search engine results pages (SERPs). That said, finding the best keywords, and using them properly, helps.

Keywords are the words and phrases people use to search for things online. By using keywords in your content, you help search engines recognize that your page matches what someone is looking for. This increases the odds that it will appear in the results of their search.

Before you start writing, do some keyword research. There are plenty of sites to help you with this task. My favourites include:

- Google's Keyword Planner

- Ahref's Keyword Explorer

- Moz's Keyword Explorer

- Ubersuggest

When it comes to finding the best keywords, there's a learning curve but it's not rocket science. Just search "how to do keyword research". I guarantee that tons of helpful pages will appear. *And remember that learning new things can be fun!*

For the most part, picking keywords is about getting into the headspace of your ideal reader—the person you most want to communicate with. Ponder what they're looking for in concrete terms: who, what, where, and why.

Keep in mind that people often add phrases and questions, like "how to", "where to", or "ways to", to their searches. Keyword phrases, also known as long-tail keywords, are common, especially when using voice search.

And don't worry about popularity so much as *specificity*.

Avoid generic keywords that are used by everyone and their dog. Instead, hone in on more specific words and phrases. These may be used in fewer searches, but the people who find you using those words are probably a better match for your content.

For example, let's say you're creating a resource to help new content writers find their niche. Using "content writing" as your main keyword is vague. That subject is broad as an ocean—and your brand-new content will likely be swallowed up in the waves.

Consider trying something more specific, like:

- Content writing niches for beginners

- How to find your niche as a content writer

- Popular niches for content writers

Fewer people may be using those phrases, but that means less competition! And when someone searches "how to find your niche as a content writer" and unearths your resource, they're more likely to appreciate it because you're giving them exactly what they're looking for.

Once you've made your keyword choices, relax and write. Keep them in mind, but don't obsess about how many times you manage to squeeze those words into your content.

In fact, trying to stuff keywords into every second sentence is a big no-no. Search engines punish pages that practise keyword stuffing. *And besides annoying the Google Gods, using the same phrases over and over makes your writing intolerable to readers.*

The key is to weave keywords into the body of your content, where they fit most organically. Then, when you're polishing your writing, strategically add them to high profile locations, like your title, the first sentence, and maybe a sub-heading.

Most of all, make sure the piece itself is high quality and matches with what your reader was searching for. **Write for *real* people, not search engines.**

CHAPTER 14
Find Your Angle

I took an art class where the first evening was all about drawing a bowl of fruit. Fourteen diligent students, including me, drew for an hour. The only noise in the room was an occasional squeaking and scraping, as one lone student shuffled her chair from spot to spot. It was a bit distracting.

Class ended with everyone displaying their work to the group. As I walked around, I noticed that some folks managed to shade more depth into their apples, but other than that, the sketches were largely interchangeable. Except for the chair shuffler.

Her sketch was a sort of aerial view. Same fruit. Same bowl. But completely unique from the other 13 sketches, and wildly more interesting!

Most often, your topic will be like that fruit bowl—already familiar to your audience in some way. Chances are high that the online universe is overflowing with content that covers the same subject. So, your job isn't to reinvent the fruit bowl; it's to move the chair.

Find an interesting perspective, a new angle, or a fresh detail. Keep moving until you find it. Start by asking yourself a few questions:

- Who's reading this and what kind of information are they looking for?

- What makes this topic important to them?

- What are all the different elements of this topic? (Ponder sub-topics and niches.)

Your answers may put a few limits on where you can place the chair. *Yes, I'm hanging onto that analogy!*

For instance, if you're writing a general interest piece for a broad audience, there will be tons of possible angles and broad freedom to play with tone, style, and language. But if your readers are already knowledgeable about the subject matter, and they're looking for specific, detailed, or technical information, you're in a tighter space.

Let's say you're writing about social media and your audience is start-ups and entrepreneurs looking for quick tips. There are *so many places* to put that chair. You could:

- Find a real-life example of a small brand that killed the competition by acing social. *Folks love a David versus Goliath story.*

- Take a humorous approach and showcase some over-the-top social media failures. *Remember to be funny— not mean. Meanness is a no-no.*

- Identify one common problem newbies tend to have with social. Hone in on that one thing. *I once wrote an entire article about when to use happy face emojis and it did great.*

Now, let's say your audience is already social-savvy and looking for technical knowledge. Storytelling and humour may not work, but you could try other things:

- Take a new angle, like risk management, or how to create a social media policy for employees.

- Dive deep. Find the latest facts and figures, take a serious tone, and go 3,000+ words. *Own* that topic with authority.

- Add resources, like policy templates and checklists, to make your piece extra helpful.

At the end of the day, it's all about creativity. Every writer sees the fruit bowl. Creative writers move the chair.

CHAPTER 15
Map Things Out

**"Organizing is what you do before you do something,
so that when you do it, it is not all mixed up."**

A. A. Milne, Author and Creator of Winnie-the-Pooh

Inside your brain, thoughts, ideas, and knowledge swirl around in strange, abstract ways. Rather than letting discombobulated information spill onto the page, it's wise to map things out before you start writing. Making an outline saves both your time and your sanity.

The structure of your outline will depend on many factors, including the desired word count, the complexity of your topic, the intended reader, the purpose of the piece, and the style of writing. For example, the outline for an in-depth white paper is going to be more formal and prescribed than the outline for a general interest blog post.

That said, the purpose remains consistent. Your goal is to chart an easy path from beginning to end, so that readers pick up the most important points and don't get lost in the weeds.

If you're struggling with layout, chances are you've got a content problem. This is another argument in favour of the outline—it's like an early warning system.

For instance, if your outline feels sparce, the content is likely too thin. You may need to do more research and increase your depth of understanding on the subject. Conversely, if your outline is monstrously long, the topic may be too broad. Ask yourself if you should niche down, or maybe break this giant diatribe into several smaller pieces of writing.

Lastly, remember that it's just a map, not a travel guide, so don't sink too deeply into the details. Making an outline is about organizing more so than writing. Save your creativity for the first draft!

CHAPTER 16
Consider the Inverted Pyramid

For those of you who haven't heard of the Inverted Pyramid, let me start by telling you that it's *not* a yoga pose.

The Inverted Pyramid is a content writing format where you lead with the most important information. It ensures that readers get your main point even if they don't read all your magical words. And online readers are notorious for skimming, so the Inverted Pyramid is well-suited to writing for the web.

Information readers MUST have for your content to serve its purpose

Helpful, but not crucial, information

Nice little extras

Following this design also makes it easier to edit and reduce your word count, because paragraphs are less and less important as you move down. It's easier to trim the fat when you know exactly where you put it!

To write content using the Inverted Pyramid approach, you need to:

- **Clearly identify your key takeaway.** What's the most important thing you're trying to communicate? Completing this sentence can be helpful: *"If readers only remembered _____, I'd be happy."*

- **Create an outline that puts your thoughts and facts in order.** Start with broad stroke information that has the strongest general appeal. Work down to smaller, more targeted details.

- **Be brutally concise.** The Inverted Pyramid style only works if the content is strong and on-point. No meandering. Favour simple language, keep your sentences and paragraphs short, and use formats like bulleted lists to cut to the chase quickly.

Within the body of your content, you can also use mini-pyramids to support that strong-and-on-point vibe. Make sure the first sentence of each paragraph shares the most important information. And put the most value-loaded words at the start of each sentence. For example, let's look at this sentence on adult literacy:

"According to the *Final Report of the International Adult Literacy Survey*, released in 2000 by the OECD and Statistics Canada, 48% of adult

Canadians have literacy skills that fall below a high school level, which has a negative impact on their ability to function and progress, both professionally and personally."[2]

This behemoth of a sentence has several problems. It's too long. It's boring. And the writer buried the lead. So, let's reconfigure things:

"Forty-eight percent of adult Canadians have literacy skills that fall below a high school level, according to a 2000 report released by the OECD and Statistics Canada. This negatively impacts on their ability to function, both at work and personally."

It could use more tweaking, but this is a stronger sentence. It packs more punch because it starts with the most important (and interesting) fact.

My only criticism of the Inverted Pyramid is that it can be challenging to create a powerful ending when you've put all the best, meatiest stuff at the beginning. Particularly in longer pieces, I like to save something impactful, like an interesting fact or quote, for my final paragraph. *Like a fruit-on-the-bottom yogourt cup. Extra delicious!*

Always remember that writing styles, principles, and templates are just tools in your writer's toolbox. You get to decide when and how to use them.

---

[2] https://abclifeliteracy.ca/literacy-at-a-glance/, accessed June 30, 2021.

CHAPTER 17
Reduce Stress with the Bite-Size Morsels Approach

Staring at a blank screen is daunting, and the more words you're trying to create, the more intimidating all that white space becomes. I find it calming to break the job down into smaller tasks.

For example, let's say your topic is "How to Beat Writer's Block" and you need to squeeze out 1,500 words. Try breaking this task into bite-size morsels:

- Write 100-150 words about why it can be hard to write content.

- Add on 100-150 words about the things that trigger writer's block.

- Compose 100-150 words about the counter-productive things people sometimes do when they have writer's block.

- Create a list of ten ways to beat writer's block, then write 100 words about each trick.

- End with 100-150 words summarizing the ten tricks.

See what I mean? Once you break it down, the intimidation level drops.

The bite-size morsels approach works for almost any topic. All you need to do is map it out, then follow the path from beginning to end. Because this is a utilitarian, mechanical method, your rough draft may seem a bit flat, but you can fix that during the editing phase.

Just to let you know, I used this approach to write my book because the thought of putting so many words together was overwhelming. To take the pressure off, I started by coming up with a list of 100 pearls of wisdom that related to content writing.

Each day, I wrote about one pearl and only 100 workdays later… I had a collection of more than 30,000 slightly flat words begging to be sorted and edited. *That was a whole* other *kind of overwhelming, but the point is that I got the words out.*

It wasn't pretty, but it was effective. I made it across the finish line by breaking a big, ambitious goal into smaller tasks that felt do-able, and you can too. Whether you're trying to write 1,500 words or 15,000, this approach works. I promise.

CHAPTER 18
Be Alert for Accidental Plagiarism

Research is an important part of content writing, and research involves reading stuff other folks have written. Learning from others is good. Stealing their words is not.

High school essay rules still apply: Always give credit when you quote someone, add footnotes when you take facts and figures from a specific source, and don't cut and paste existing content into your own. But in the grown-up world of content writing, avoiding plagiarism can be way more complicated.

Let's say you're writing about widgets and how to use them properly. Before creating the world's greatest widget-related content, you need to know exactly what widgets do, what problems they solve, hazards and risks, regulations, alternatives, and what do to when widget activities go wrong. There's a vast universe of widget wisdom begging to be explored!

A thousand years later…

You're ready to write. But now your brain's full of other people's words and every sentence you create sounds vaguely familiar. *Arghhh!*

The best thing you can do at this point is stop writing. Go for a walk. Make a cup of coffee. Or tea. Or wine. *No judgment.*

Give yourself enough time to have thoughts that aren't related to widgets. This is important because those unrelated thoughts are *true* to you. They put your own voice back in the driver's seat.

When you're ready, start again, and follow these tips to avoid accidental plagiarism:

- **Read from lots of different sources.** Working from a broader collection of information makes it easier to create content that's both accurate and original.

- **Use links.** If someone has already explained something perfectly, that's great. Don't waste time reinventing the wheel, just give them credit. In online writing, the simplest way to do this is to link to their content. *Easy-peasy. And respectful.*

- **Edit. Edit. Edit.** Each round of edits gives you another opportunity to polish your words and say things in a way that's more authentic.

Most of all, **be honest with yourself.** You know when you've written something using your own words, and deep down, you know when you've cheated. There's a fine line between paraphrasing and plagiarizing. If you feel like even your baby toe has stepped over that line, link to the source of your wisdom!

PART 3
Get the Words Out

Sometimes the words come easy; sometimes they don't. Creating a warm, welcoming space to do your thing helps. Understanding your purpose, your audience, and your topic helps. But there is no secret formula.

At some point, you need to hunker down with your fingers on a keyboard and your eyeballs on a screen. And whether it brings you joy or agony, you must write.

Squeezing a mass of words out of your head is messy work. They may splatter like gobs of paint on a canvas and mix in ways you didn't expect. Or they may come out in tiny, colourless drops that sit flat and isolated from one another.

The only path forward is to keep squeezing. One way or another, your job is to get those words onto the page so you can start shaping them into something spectacular.

Getting the words out is about creating, not refining, so don't fret over details, like where to put the commas. That said, as you become more skilled and confident as a writer, sentence structure and punctuation naturally improve, and first drafts tend to come out cleaner. *Another great reason to keep expanding your repertoire of writing strategies and techniques!*

In this section, I'm going to explain a few principles and practices that will help you create a first draft that's relatively coherent and has a bit of style already in place.

CHAPTER 19
Set a Timer

Does this sound familiar?

The words are stuck in your head. It's like swimming through mud. The clock is ticking but you refuse to surrender. An hour passes. Then another hour. Arghhh!

Or this:

You're INTO it. Sure, you've veered off topic, or burrowed deep into a rabbit hole. But your creativity is on fire—and it's merrily burning through your day.

Or God forbid, this:

Content writing is on your to-do list, but it never gets to-done. In fact, it never gets started.

Whether you're writing short, promotional copy, or a deep-dive article, time can still be a problem. It's hard to find and even harder to control. That's where the timer comes in. It's not sexy, but it works.

Discipline and routine aren't the antithesis of creativity; they're guardians of your creative process. A timer forces you to start and reminds you to stop. It helps you develop focus and control, and it protects you from both procrastination and burnout.

Timer Tips:

- **Don't over-commit.** You'll be surprised how much you can get done in a short but focused block of time. I frequently start with just 30 minutes on the clock.

- **Stop while you're ahead.** If you get into a creative groove, and your schedule isn't too busy, it's okay to start that timer one more time. But don't keep chewing through your day. It defeats the purpose of establishing discipline and routine.

- **Don't allow interruptions.** This is your writing time, so don't check your email, take a "quick peek" at social media, or answer that phone call. Those things can wait.

In the words of entrepreneur, author and motivational speaker, Jim Rohn, "**Either you run the day, or the day runs you.**"

The timer is your friend!

CHAPTER 20
Understand the Psychology of Words

"Words and magic were in the beginning one and the same thing, and even today, words retain much of their magical power."

Sigmund Freud, the Father of Modern Psychology

When you talk to someone, you use words, but you also lean into tone, body language, and facial expressions. It's a whole *thing*. When you write, there are only words.

That said, if you pick the right words and you play with them creatively, you can establish a mood, make readers *feel* things, and build rapport, as surely as a speaker on a stage. It's magical.

The secret to tapping into the magical power of language is to appreciate that **every word has both a meaning and a personality.**

Think of something as simple as "hi" versus "hello". They mean the same thing. But "hi" is how friends greet each other, whereas "hello" is what a high-priced consultant says when they meet a prospective client.

"Hi" has a warm, cheery personality, so it's the best choice if you want your writing to have a casual, friendly tone. But if you're creating an authority piece or your subject is serious, "hello" may serve you better. It's not pretentious, but it has a more distinguished personality.

I'm a huge fan of the online thesaurus. It's a great tool for finding new, interesting words. But before I replace any word with a synonym, I ask myself what the original word feels like to readers, and whether the new option has the same vibe.

For example, based on meaning alone, you could replace the word "interesting" with either "gripping" or "enchanting". Obviously, the emotional response of readers would be very different, depending on your choice.

Words evoke feelings. So does composition. And the more you understand about how the human brain works, the easier it is to create content that grabs attention and impacts readers.

For instance, did you know that the brain can only hold on to four items at a time? When speaking, that converts to one or two sentences. So, what happens if your writing is filled with strings of complicated sentences fused into giant paragraphs?

Well, the first problem is that most readers lose the thread. Even if the topic is fascinating and your words are brilliant, they're doomed. By the time they struggle to the end of a paragraph, the first sentence is already fading.

The second, bigger problem is that not being able to understand something makes people feel bad. Confused. Dumb. And no one likes those feelings. In that kind of situation, online readers do what human nature (a.k.a. psychology) dictates—they click away.

Here's another cool tidbit about how the brain reacts to words:

When you use a single word to describe something, the brain quickly brings that action or object to mind. But unnecessary text induces skipping. The brain struggles to connect the longer phrase with something *real*, so it gives up and moves on.

Compare these two sentences:

- They grabbed a pen.

You can easily see this in your mind.

- They quickly reached for a pen.

This is blurrier.

"Grab" is visceral. You *feel* it. "Quickly reached" is more cerebral. You intellectually understand the motion, but you don't *feel* it as intensely.

As a writer, you need to keep adjectives and adverbs on a short leash because the psychology of words tells us that clear and simple is best. It makes it easier for readers to understand your writing. Moreover, it makes them feel smart. That's a big deal, because feeling smart makes the brain happy, and a happy brain keeps reading!

CHAPTER 21
Speak Like a Human

A person stuck in a well doesn't request "assistance", "support", or "facilitation". They holler for HELP! This applies whether the person in the well is a teenager, an academic, or a corporate executive.

Most of the time, when we're trying to communicate with other humans, we grab the simplest, most familiar words—the ones that are front-of-mind. We save the giant, imposing words for situations where we are trying to impress others.

Content that's overflowing with formal, over-wrought language, doesn't necessarily come across as smart to readers. More likely, the vibe is that the writer is trying to sound smart, and that's not the vibe you want. Ever.

Keep it simple and speak like a human.

CHAPTER 22
Use Contractions with Care

In real life, we use contractions, so they're an easy way to make your writing more personable and friendly. That said, some audiences find them hard to understand.

For example, readers with learning disabilities, or readers who have English as a second language, may struggle to process contractions.

Complex contractions, like could've, would've, and should've, are especially hard to read. Frankly, they're a mouthful! And there's something *slangy* about the sound of them.

On the other hand, simple, positive contractions, like it's, you'll, and they're, don't cause as much confusion. So, if you're writing for a general audience and want a down-to-earth sort of tone, simple contractions can do the trick.

The important thing is to think about the people most likely to read your content. Put yourself in their shoes and focus on making your words readable and relatable for *them*.

CHAPTER 23
Use Fragments. Sometimes.

"Grammar is a piano I play by ear."

Joan Didion, Writer

By definition, a sentence must have three things: a subject, a verb, and a complete thought. A sentence fragment is missing one of these critical components. It's an incomplete sentence.

Most writing handbooks (and high school English teachers) view sentence fragments as mistakes. *I agree. Sometimes.*

Careless disregard for the rules of grammar is unacceptable. It's a sign of lazy writing. But deliberately using a fragment is not a mistake; it's a creative choice.

If you want to sound polished and professional, stick to full sentences. But if you're aiming for a more relaxed, conversational tone, sentence fragments are your friends.

For example:

Full sentence: We're happy to help you.
Sentence fragment: Happy to help.

The difference is subtle, but significant. "We're happy to help you" carries more authority but "happy to help" is warmer.

In general, avoid fragments when writing formal, scholarly content. Full sentences sound more intellectual. *Consistent use of full sentences is the written equivalent of putting on horn-rimmed glasses.*

That said, intellectual isn't always better. In fact, the purpose of most online content is not to show people how smart you are—it's to communicate, connect, and share valuable information.

In verbal conversations, sentence fragments are as common as full sentences. So, if you want to build rapport with readers, sentence fragments are a useful tool.

Remember that you're in charge.

If your high school English teacher takes up content writing as a side hustle, they can be as picky as they like about the structure of their sentences. But when it's *your* fingers on the keyboard, banish their judgmental voice from your head!

Make your own choices. If a few well-placed fragments suit your purpose, use them.

The key is to be deliberate. Know the difference between a full sentence and a fragment. And don't go overboard. There's a fine line between casual and sloppy.

CHAPTER 24
Lean Into the Positive

**"The benefits often outweigh the suffering.
Never concentrate on the pain, focus on the reward."**

Lailah Gifty Akita, Inspirational Writer

As a content writer, you can't be a Sally Sunshine all the time. Your topic may be serious, sad, or even scary, and the tone of your writing must respect the facts.

That said, if the purpose of your content is to help readers, teach them something, or inspire them to do something, you get better long-term results from positivity than negativity. Remember your favourite teacher from back in elementary school? *I guarantee that teacher knew how to lean into the positive!*

When your language and tone are positive, readers feel confident, capable, and respected. They relax. And they embrace your message rather than resist it.

To make your writing more persuasive, be conscious of how you phrase things. Think DOs instead of DON'Ts. Read these two sentences:

Option 1: You won't be able to reach your financial goals until you figure out how to budget.

Option 2: You'll be able to reach your financial goals as soon as you figure out how to budget.

Option 1 is depressing, but option 2 feels like I might be able to handle it. *Sure, I can figure things out!*

Whenever possible, frame concepts to highlight upsides over downsides. Re-framing isn't about changing the facts. Often, it's just about leaning toward optimism rather than pessimism. Consider:

- 50% chance of failure.

- 50% chance of success!

Obviously, the math is the same. But the risk of failure hits hard, while the possibility of success is inherently inspiring.

When you must present negative information, consider ways to buffer the downside with a positive or two. For example:

- The solution to this problem is expensive.

- There's a solution to this problem. It's expensive, but it <u>will</u> fix things.

Maybe I'm okay with spending a little money if the outcome is going to fix my problem!

Full disclosure: There are times when putting a negative spin on something works better, or at least faster. But the short-term gain may come with a long-term downside.

For example, let's say you're writing about a famine, and you want readers to donate money right away. Playing into negative emotions, like fear and guilt, may spur folks into action, which would be a positive result. But that one-time donation may not lead to long-term support for your cause, because fear inspires both action and avoidance.

Sometimes it's hard to lean into the positive. In fact, it may challenge your creativity and your writing skills. But it's worth the effort because **great writing doesn't coerce—it convinces.**

CHAPTER 25
Connect with You-and-I Language

The intention of your writing should be to both communicate *and* connect because this makes your message more impactful, and because communication without connection is boring.

Ponder this promotional statement for a book:

- The purpose of this book is to help readers improve their writing skills and confidence.

There's nothing inherently wrong with this sentence, but it's dry. Let's try it again with a few less words and a "you":

- This book will help you improve your writing skills and confidence.

This is more interesting because it mentions *you* instead of a nebulous blob of *readers*. So, let's pour more you-and-I into the mix and see what happens:

- Want to improve your writing skills and confidence? In this book, I'll show you how.

Feel the difference? Now we're having a conversation. You see yourself. You also see me offering to help you. We're connected. *It also helps to use a question, but we'll get into that technique in the next chapter.*

One of the easiest, most effective ways to create connection is to use you-and-I language. It's natural and conversational. If you were talking to someone face-to-face, you wouldn't call them "person", or "client", or "reader". That would be weird. It would make you sound like a robot.

On the page, you can get away with those generic terms, but the effect is still a bit off-putting. It creates a distance between you and the reader. Switching to you-and-I language bridges that divide and forges a stronger personal connection.

Let's say you're creating content for a brand. Check out these options:

Warm*ish*:   ABC Inc. creates the best widgets in the universe. Our clients love them.

Warm: We create the best widgets in the universe. You'll love them.

Using personal pronouns is a game-changer: "WE create widgets for YOU"!

The secret is to **write like you're speaking to an audience of one**. Focus on that one person and talk to them as though you're seated beside them on a sofa. They know you. You know them.

CHAPTER 26
Ask Purposeful Questions

I had a friend who asked a million questions. Maybe I should have been flattered by his keen interest in my life and my thoughts. But truthfully, I found him exhausting. *Hence the past tense.*

I feel the same way about content that's littered with questions. Used in moderation, they can be engaging and persuasive, and may make people think more deeply about your message. But not all questions are equally effective and relying on questions to do the heavy lifting can appear gimmick-y.

The key to using questions effectively is to be careful and deliberate. Make sure each one is clear, persuasive, and serves a purpose.

Clear questions are engaging, but they don't require readers to think *too* hard. For example:

- "What would you do?" is thought-provoking.

- "Would you do X? Or Y? Or Z?" is confusing.

Persuasive questions spark agreement. For example, let's say you're writing about tropical vacations and your audience is Canadian:

- "Do you hate winter?" may sound like a great starter question, but what if the reader loves winter? *Oops. Now they're clicking away to look for ski holidays!*

- "Dreaming about the perfect winter escape?" is better because it's safe to assume that someone who's searching for content about tropical vacations wants to go on one.

Purposeful questions serve the content in some way. Perhaps you want readers to ponder something important. Or maybe you just want to add a conversational spark. Both of these purposes are worthy.

There's nothing wrong with adding clear, persuasive, purposeful questions to a piece of content. In fact, they can be a lovely addition. But don't go overboard.

Too much of a good thing is still, well… too much.

CHAPTER 27
Tell Stories

**"We are, as a species, addicted to story.
Even when the body goes to sleep, the mind
stays up all night, telling itself stories."**

Jonathan Gottschall, Literary Scholar

As a parent, I've got stories for *everything*. For example, my daughters became passionate about brushing their teeth after hearing the story of my poor cousin who ate marshmallows every night and wound up with dentures as a teen. *I'll skip the details, but it's a gruesome tale.*

We associate storytelling with fiction, but in truth, stories are an intricate part of our daily lives. We tell stories to explain things, to support our opinions, to spice up our conversations, and to share elements of ourselves with others. Storytelling is a great way to turn abstract notions, like dental hygiene, into feel-able concepts that linger in the mind.

The basics of storytelling are simple. You have a protagonist, some sort of conflict or problem, and a general structure (beginning + middle + end). Think about the case studies you see on company websites. These are just true-life stories about someone with a problem and how they solved it by using a particular product, process, or service.

> Company ABC (the protagonist) was struggling to get new customers (the problem). They had invested tons of time and money on their website and created mountains of content, but it wasn't translating into more business. They came to us for help. We did *yada yada yada* (middle/plot/action). Within a year, they were able to expand into three new countries (happy ending)!

This isn't a bad story. But whether it sits politely on the page or jumps up and grabs you depends on the writer. And that's why storytelling is an ART.

If it were me, I might replace that company name with a real person. Make the problem more visceral.

> Bob was stressed. He'd gone deep into a new website design and content development, but the results were lukewarm. Online traffic was flat and so were sales.

I might also bring that happy ending into better focus. Make it something more tangible that folks might recognize as a personal success rather than a corporate one.

> Bob's story has a happy ending! Today, his company has expanded into three new countries and he's planning vacations instead of stressing.

Note: Pulling a case study off a website and jazzing it up is a great writing exercise. Set a timer for 20 minutes and see what you can accomplish.

My favourite form of storytelling is the personal anecdote. Leading with a snippet from my own life is an effective way to set the scene and build a quick rapport with readers. I've used this technique quite a few times in this book, including at the beginning of this chapter.

A fussy writer might argue that these little snippets aren't true stories because they're super short and lack a fully fleshed out structure. And they would be right—technically.

But when it comes to storytelling, the *art* part is far more important than the structure part.

At its heart, storytelling is about tapping into emotions and connecting with readers. To do that, all you need is:

- A relatable protagonist (like a mom trying to get her kids to brush their teeth)

- Strong, visceral language (like "gruesome")

- A story that makes sense in the context of what you're writing about

Once upon a time there was a content writer who mastered the art of storytelling. The people gobbled up the writer's magic words with glee and learned all kinds of important things from them. The content writer basked in the glory of their own brilliance and lived happily ever after. The End.

CHAPTER 28
Don't Just Name Feelings. Create Them.

You can't make someone happy by telling them to be happy. Happiness doesn't work that way, nor do any of the other subtle and not-so-subtle feelings in the universe of human emotions.

My poor hubby is notorious for trying to put me in a good mood by pre-emptively announcing that I'm going to love something. *Whenever he does this, I'm immediately suspicious that he's foreshadowing a deadly dull event.*

Lazy writers do the same thing. They lead with proclamations like:

- You'll be happy/sad/thrilled/appalled to know…

- Here's the best/worst part…

- We've got exciting news to share…

Readers immediately sense dullness and disappointment coming, and they're seldom wrong. *Don't fall into the trap of over-hyping and under-delivering.*

In general, it's best to avoid naming feelings or telling people how to feel. At best, it's ineffective, and at worst, it's pushy. Instead, focus on *creating* feelings. Sprinkle powerful words into the imagination of the reader and let the magic happen.

This isn't as hard as you might think. The next time you write down a feeling-name, like "happy", stop to ponder that emotion. What does it *look* like?

For instance, people who are happy might:

- Smile or grin

- Giggle or laugh

- Hum or sing

- Dance around

- Jump, bounce, skip, or leap

- Clap their hands

- Hug and kiss

When you can *see* happiness in your own mind, start conjuring up words to help readers see it too. Then swap out the word "happy" for a more visceral option.

"You'll be happy to know..." might become:

- You'll grin ear-to-ear...

- You'll smile all day...

- You'll be hopping, skipping, and jumping...

There's life and vibrancy to these statements. They're a little corny, so they may not work in every situation, but they're a solid starting point. And once you're thinking about what makes people grin ear-to-ear, your creativity is apt to kick into high gear. For example, you might feel inspired to add a story to your writing about how you made someone grin ear-to-ear.

The best part of being a writer is making people feel things, so don't skip it. Instead, burrow deeply into it. Let your inner writer *see* the feelings and *play* with the words.

CHAPTER 29
Consider Breaking the Fourth Wall

Breaking the Fourth Wall is a storytelling technique in which the writer or a character speaks directly to the audience. Think of Ferris Bueller in the classic movie *Ferris Bueller's Day Off* or Ryan Reynolds' character in the *Deadpool* movies.

If neither of these examples are familiar, it's time for a movie night. Make some popcorn, curl up on your sofa, and expand your horizons!

See what's happening here?

I'm speaking directly to you. Letting you in on the action. And possibly chastising you for your lack of pop culture knowledge. This is an example of breaking the fourth wall, which is also known as an "aside".

Asides can be a very useful tool in your content writing toolbox. Done well, they add personality and pizzazz, and build a more intimate connection with readers. That said, like all tools of the trade, they should only be used when they serve the purpose of the piece.

In general:

- Asides work best when the subject is light or at least benign. They convey humour well, but deeper emotions can fall flat.

- If your word count is out of control, axe the asides. They're an extra, not a mainstay.

- And don't overdo it. Using too many asides can frustrate readers who just want you to get to the point.

I frequently break the fourth wall to keep readers engaged in otherwise dry topics. *Like in this chapter, where I'm working with the not-very-fun-or-flirty topic of asides.*

Hope it worked!

CHAPTER 30
Respect the Rule of Three

"Well, it's one for the money, two for the show, three to get ready now go, cat, go."

Elvis Presley, the King of Rock and Roll

We humans easily remember things that come in threes. When you add more items, our retention nosedives. Perhaps because of this, we also tend to like the look of things that are grouped in threes, whether it's three candles on a mantlepiece or three items on a list.

Experienced writers (and interior designers) use the rule of three to attract the eye, hold attention, and amplify impact.

Read that sentence again, please.

Can you feel the rhythm of "attract the eye, hold attention, and amplify impact"? That's the magic of three.

There are many ways to use the rule of threes to your advantage. For example:

- **When possible, use three bullet points in a list.** Two is lame and four or more is sometimes overwhelming. But three feels just right.

- **Break a long or complex process into three steps.** It will seem more manageable to readers.

- **Highlight three main points in your conclusion or summary.** This helps readers retain the things you most want them to remember.

The rule of three is particularly important when your purpose is to inform, educate, or inspire. Always ask yourself: What do I really need people to remember? Use the rule of three to reinforce those key takeaways.

Let's suppose you're writing about a service of some sort and you've identified seven amazing benefits to that service. *Congratulations. That's a lot of benefits.*

The problem is that readers won't remember all seven benefits, no matter how magical your words are. It's a human brain limitation. *Biology, my friend. Nothing you can do about it.*

So, you must be brutal. Kill your weakest darlings. Slash that list of benefits down to three. Remember that the purpose of your writing is *not* to show people how smart you are or how much you know about something. It's to communicate effectively and with purpose.

Do you want them to forget seven benefits? Or clearly remember three?

CHAPTER 31
Use Humour with Caution

**"Analyzing humour is like dissecting a frog.
Few people are interested, and the frog dies of it."**

E. B. White, Essayist, Author, Humourist, and Poet

Humour in writing is a tricky thing. You're crafting it with only words and tone. No body language. No sound effects.

When it works, it's a powerful force. Humour can spice up dry topics, lighten the tone, and build a beautiful rapport between you and your audience. But when it fails, it's like farting in a car. There's nowhere to hide, and everyone knows it was you.

Note: Farting in a car can be funny! But only if the right people are in the car with you.

That's the thing about humour. Things are not simply funny or *not* funny. The effect is only partially about what you say. In fact, it's often more about how you say it, and who you say it to.

So, before you start dropping one-liners into any piece of writing, think about how that joke or comment fits within the context of the topic. Consider how it may be interpreted by the people most likely to read it. Make sure the funny bits suit your audience, your subject matter, and your tone.

Here are a few guidelines when it comes to humour:

- **Be strategic.** Don't overdo it. Humour is like hot sauce. A little adds pep and pizzazz, but one drop too much and people put down their forks.

- **Keep it focused.** Don't veer off topic just to squeeze in some funny. Every element of your writing should serve your purpose. Irrelevant observations and jokes are a waste of word count and disconcerting to readers.

- **Focus on yourself and *your* foibles.** Anecdotes and witty observations work best when they're personal. Laughing at yourself is funny; laughing at someone else is not.

Most importantly, **be wary of first draft humour.** Like everything else in a first draft, it's raw, and raw humour sometimes veers a little too close to sarcasm.

During the edit process, review each bit of funny text carefully. If your inner critic smells a fart, hit delete!

CHAPTER 32
Limit Your Use of Acronyms

Damn all the things with giant long names!

I suspect that government leaders, scientists, and tech folks compete to see how many words they can put into a title.

Monstrous, lengthy terms are a common annoyance for content writers. They're boring, they devour your word count, and they drain the peppiness out of perfectly decent sentences.

Enter acronyms, those clever little word and letter combinations that condense things into tidy packages. Thanks to acronyms, you need not waste 20 characters writing "for your information" when FYI will do the trick!

Problem solved.

Alas, like so many quick fixes, using acronyms can have unwanted side effects:

- They confuse folks who don't know what those letter combinations represent.

- They muck up the flow of your writing almost as much as the terms you're trying to avoid.

- And if you overdo it, your content can end up looking like alphabet soup.

To minimize confusion and keep readers in the loop, **write terms out the first time, even if they're long and unwieldy.** Introduce the acronym using brackets. After that, you can start using the acronym on its own.

Example: "According to the World Health Organization (WHO)…"

If you're confident that readers know the acronym, you can disregard this rule. For instance, if your audience is Canadian, you don't need to spell out Royal Canadian Mounted Police because everyone in the country says RCMP. But if you're writing for an international audience, you should follow the rule and spell it out once.

I also recommend reading sentences with acronyms aloud at least once, and twice if you've got time. It's especially important to *hear* sentences involving acronyms, abbreviations, and technical terms because how they look and how they sound can be very different.

For example, "A RCMP officer reported…" looks okay upon first glance. But when you try to read it aloud, there's an awkward stutter because your tongue has trouble jumping from the "A" to the "R". Change to "An RCMP officer reported…" and that awkwardness goes away.

Note: In general, you add articles (a/an) to acronyms based on what they sound like, not how they're spelled. So, if the first sound is a consonant, put an "a" in front, but if it's a vowel sound (like that soft "arrrrr" at the beginning of RCMP), use "an".

Applied thoughtfully, acronyms are a helpful, and sometimes necessary, writing tool. But they're not real words; they're just substitutes for real words. So, keep them to a minimum.

You don't want to end up with alphabet soup!

CHAPTER 33
Be Persuasive Not Pushy

"You cannot antagonize and influence at the same time."

John Knox, Minister, Theologian, and Writer

As a mother, I've spent a significant portion of my life trying to steer uncooperative offspring through routine activities. These experiences have made one thing abundantly clear: **Pushy doesn't work. Persuasive does.**

Here's an example from the world of parenting:

Pushy: Brush your teeth or you'll be sorry! *(This is the classic don't-make-me-pull-this-car-over strategy.)*

Persuasive: Let's all brush our teeth now and get it over with.

Even better: Let's all brush our teeth so we can relax and watch that show you've been raving about! *(Arguably, this involves bribery, but bribery works so I stand by it.)*

Readers are like children. They generally resist being told what to do, so it's important to consciously check your language. It's fine to be assertive, but aggressive is a turn-off.

Subtle differences in your word choices can make a big difference in terms of how your message is received. Here are a few tips to keep from crossing that fine line between persuasive and pushy:

- Whenever possible, replace uber-forceful words, like do/don't or must/must not, with softer alternatives, like consider, think about, or choose. For example:

  Pushy: You must do this.
  Persuasive: Think about doing this.

  If you're writing an instructional piece, like a how-to article, and softer words feel too wishy washy, another option is to use passive, process-related words.

  Neutral: Your first step is to _____.
                  Begin by _____.

  This isn't persuasive writing, but it doesn't hit readers over the head either. The effect is benign.

- Beware of the word "should". It's both judge-y and over-used. Often, simply removing it from a sentence improves the tone.

  Judge-y: To accomplish this goal, you should consider doing _____.
  Less judge-y: To accomplish this goal, consider doing _____.

It's amazing how many of the extra, unnecessary words we unconsciously add to our writing are judge-y or pushy.

- Keep a tight leash on exclamation points and font gimmicks. **DON'T SCREAM COMMANDS IN GIANT PRINT WITH BOLD CAPITAL LETTERS!!**

No one enjoys being hit over the head with advice or opinions, so it's always better to persuade than push. Rather than relying on aggressive language, use things like examples, statistics, and authority quotes to add strength to your advice and opinions. This approach lets readers form their own conclusions, albeit the ones you want them to form.

CHAPTER 34
Remember that Clear Outshines Clever

"The three most important elements in non-fiction writing are: clarity, clarity, and clarity."

Ayn Rand, Writer and Philosopher

Writers love to be clever. It's in our DNA. We yearn to create intricate patterns of words that make folks *feel* something.

We enjoy crafting a story. Adding a narrative. Tickling the reader with a bit of clever wordplay. And there's nothing wrong with these desires unless we allow them to run amok.

The purpose of writing content is to communicate. It's not to showcase your cleverness.

If storytelling serves a purpose, go for it. If a dollop of humour is going to make a dull topic more engaging, add it. And feel free to swap dull words out for peppier alternatives. But keep your eye on the prize.

Focus on communicating clearly and succinctly, and always respect your readers. Don't test their patience with meandering passages that indulge your creativity at the expense of their time.

The best content is useful, easy to read, and enjoyable. So be creative—but keep it tight.

CHAPTER 35
Accept That First Drafts Suck

Even when you do tons of research, totally understand your audience, and know more about your topic than any other human… 99.99% of the time, your first draft will suck. And that's okay. The purpose of your first draft isn't to showcase your mastery of the English language or your creative brilliance; it's just to spit your thoughts out.

Sometimes, that pile of spit-out thoughts is only marginally disturbing to look at. Other times, it's a crime scene. But despite appearances, it's still an accomplishment.

Take the win! Congratulate yourself. Then, if possible, walk away. Whether you're feeling relieved to have created something, or frustrated by the lack of perfection, this is an ideal time to **take a break.**

DO:	Make a cup of tea. Walk the dog. Chat with a friend.
DON'T:	Start fussing over spelling mistakes, sentence structure, awkward phrases, or mismatched metaphors. All that stuff will be fixed in the editing process.

Don't stress out. The first draft is for your eyes only.

And it's probably not as grotesque as you imagine. We writers are notoriously self-critical.

PART 4
Polish Your Content

There could be a writer whose words land so perfectly on the page that no edits are required. It's theoretically possible. But so is time travel.

In real life, *all* first drafts must be tidied up and polished. Even if you're tickled pink with what you've put on the page, I guarantee that it will benefit from proper editing.

The bad (or at least slightly disheartening) news is that editing is a fussy process that requires focus. You can't skim your way through it. *Well, you can, but you won't accomplish much.*

The good news is that even mediocre content can become spectacular through edits.

And the great news is that editing can be as creative and mentally engrossing as writing! *Truthfully, it's my favourite part of the content creation process.*

Ultimately, editing is about playing with words and shaping them into something beautiful. If you approach it with a positive mindset, I promise it can be fun.

In this section, I'm going to talk about the many, many things to look for when you're editing, and how small tweaks can make a huge difference in the quality and effectiveness of your writing.

CHAPTER 36
Always Make Readers Feel Smart

**"If you can't explain it simply,
you don't understand it well enough."**

Albert Einstein, one of the greatest Physicists of all time

I once attended a conference where the keynote speaker used most of his podium time to promote a book. He described his own writing as "deep" and took pride in declaring that he made no attempt to "dumb things down" for readers.

A copy of his sacred tome was distributed to the audience and we were challenged to read it overnight. *Our due diligence would be rewarded with a Q&A on day two of the event.*

In the spirit of full disclosure, I must admit to ordering wine with my room service meal, so maybe I wasn't at my intellectual best. But WOW! That book redefined boring.

I couldn't get through it. And I was definitely his target audience. *I'd already spent my hard-earned money to listen to him drone on about this EXACT topic.*

So, was that my failure? Or his?

Reading should never be a chore.

Even if the topic is challenging and there's a steep learning curve, readers should feel capable of making the climb. And if they don't, it's your problem, not theirs. Period.

You make readers feel smart when you:

- Tell them something new or put a new twist on something.

- Stick to the topic.

- Use clear, simple language.

- Use analogies and examples to help explain and simplify things.

- Break complicated processes into steps.

- Use images and illustrations to help visual learners.

- Add headings and sub-headings to break long pieces of content into smaller, more digestible morsels.

Smart writing nurtures smart readers. Your job as a writer is masterfully use words to bring your topic to life and command attention. There are no *dumb* readers, just *bored* ones.

CHAPTER 37
Tidy Up. Play. Decorate. Revisit.

In my experience, it takes at least four rounds of edits to turn a mass of sentences into a polished piece of writing. Here's the general process:

Round 1: Tidy Up

Break giant masses of writing into short, concise paragraphs. Organize the flow with sub-headings if that fits the format. Make sure you've covered the subject properly, then delete sentences that feel repetitive or off-topic.

Note: Tidying up is the least fun part of editing. It's the creative equivalent to housecleaning—a long, dull slog, but it feels great when you finish.

Round 2: Play with the Sentences

This part is so entertaining that you may need to use a timer. Otherwise, you could end up cavorting with your words all day and abandoning the other items on your to-do list. *I've done this many, many times.*

Playing with the sentences can be pure joy. It's where you get to do stuff like:

- Prune the adverbs and adjectives.

- Kill anything that smells like business-speak or jargon.

- Toss in exciting verbs that grab attention.

- Renovate passive sentences so they're active and engaging.

- Make sure you're speaking directly to your audience (use you-and-I language).

- Insert some personality!

Round 3: Decorate

Add splashes of colour and tidbits of text that leap out at your readers, like images, quotes, statistics, and links to related content. If it fits the tone and format, get a little fun and flirty. **Bold** a sentence or two. CAPITALIZE something. *Use italics.*

Round 4: Rest and Revisit

It's tempting to hit "post" or "publish" as soon as you've finished decorating. Or send it to the client if that's the scenario. Don't. It's not your fault, but at this point, you've gone so deep into the minutia that you've lost appreciation for the *whole*. As the familiar adage goes, you can't see the forest for the trees.

Instead of going for immediate gratification, press "save". Close things up and move on to something else, preferably not involving writing. The next morning, when you're properly caffeinated, read through it one more time. Ask yourself:

Does it say everything it needs to say? Is there anything that could be explained in clearer, simpler terms? Is the tone right?

If you need to make a few more tweaks, do it. Then take a deep breath and congratulate yourself on a job well done.

Enjoy your accomplishment!

CHAPTER 38
Be Wary of Editing Apps

"Perfection is just... boring. Perfect is what's natural or real; that is beauty."

Marc Jacobs, Fashion Designer

If you struggle with spelling and punctuation, online tools like Grammarly and Hemingway are the bomb. They're a great way to catch typos, missing commas, and loose threads, so your writing ends up polished and professional.

But beware the allure of perfection. Those helpful apps don't stop at spelling tweaks. They also like to dispense advice on sentence structure and word choice, and they're aggressive about getting you to acquiesce to their demands.

Sentences that displease them are underlined or highlighted in awful, gawdy colours that only disappear if you re-shape your words to match their ideals. This positions each edit as a correction—even those that are arguably subjective.

For example, a sentence that's considered too long will remain highlighted until you break it into smaller morsels, and a complicated piece of text will be targeted until you simplify the language to *their* satisfaction.

It's tempting to let them have their way every time, because it feels like you're working toward perfection. But the side of a cereal box is grammatically perfect. *Just saying.*

Don't let those cheery little algorithms pluck the voice and style out of your writing.

Keep them in their place. Remember that they're just one of the tools in your writer's toolbox. **You're the boss!**

CHAPTER 39
Make Sure it Flows

At every waterpark there's some version of a lazy river. Folks sink into inner tubes and let the current carry them along. It's a real crowd pleaser. That's *flow*.

When your writing flows well, readers don't struggle to steer, or paddle, or fight with waves. They just relax and go where the words lead them.

Most often, readers don't consciously appreciate when content has great flow, but they do recognize when it's choppy. Flow is funny that way. You notice it most when it's absent.

Here are a few tips and tricks to help maintain a good flow:

- **Vary the length of your sentences.** Variety is more interesting and engrossing. It sounds natural instead of robotic, and that makes it easier to sink into.

- **Maintain continuity of thought** from one sentence to another and from one paragraph to the next. This may sound obvious, but it's surprising how often writers randomly chop off one thought and jump to another, thereby creating the dreaded "choppiness".

- **Use transition words and phrases** to help readers move along without losing the thread. For an example, reread the first part of this chapter. *See how I used "most often" at the beginning of paragraph three? It's there to gently lead you forward.*

As a writer, your mastery of flow improves with experience. The more you write, the better you get at the nuts and bolts of putting sentences and paragraphs together, and the more you develop a *feel* for when things sound smooth.

If you get that lazy river feeling, chances are you've got decent flow. If the sensation is more akin to kayaking through rapids, keep at it. A few more transition phrases may do the trick. *And if you're wondering about how to play with your transitions, no worries. I've got a whole chapter on that!*

CHAPTER 40
Tighten Your Sentences

Take a deep breath. Now read this sentence:

> The purpose of this part of the book is to explain why a sentence that is grammatically correct, structurally accurate, and filled with important information that's valuable to readers, may still be incapable of effectively communicating that information or even holding the reader's attention.

Confused? Bored? Gasping for air?

That sentence is simply *not* readable. It's too bloody long, and there are 11 words with three or more syllables!

When we read, our brain and our eyeballs work together. The eyeballs suck up the words and feed them to the brain. The brain is very polite. It doesn't rush the eyeballs. Instead, it waits for them to pause. Then, and only then, it processes the meaning of what it's been fed.

Long, complicated sentences take longer to read and longer to make sense of. They exhaust the eyeballs and overwhelm the brain. And because no one likes to feel exhausted and overwhelmed, our natural response is to stop reading.

In your first draft, feel free to ramble, but during the editing process, you must tighten up those sentences and make them readable:

- Break long sentences into shorter ones.

- Replace long words and phrases with clearer, more succinct alternatives.

- Axe unnecessary words.

Let's use my enormous, exhausting introduction as an example. Here are a few quick fixes:

Replace => The purpose of this part of the book is to explain

With => This chapter explains

Replace => a sentence that is grammatically correct, structurally accurate, and filled with important information that's valuable to readers

With => a properly built sentence that says something worth saying

Replace => may still be incapable of effectively communicating that information

With => may still fail to make its point

Replace => or even holding the reader's attention.

With => or even hold attention.

With a bit of pruning, we can cut the word count of that monster sentence in half, and still say the same thing:

> This chapter explains why a properly built sentence that says something worth saying may still fail to make its point or even hold attention.

Not bad. But every reader knows it's a chapter, so let's axe that bit too. This leaves us with:

> A properly built sentence that says something worth saying may still fail to make its point, or even hold attention.

Now we're getting somewhere!

This text may not be bursting with personality, but it's clear, concise, and easy to read. And every sentence doesn't need to knock it out of the park, so long as they work together to win the game!

CHAPTER 41
Use Vivid Verbs

**"Every adjective and adverb is worth five cents.
Every verb is worth 50 cents."**

Mary Oliver, Pulitzer Prize-winning Poet

To be honest, I'm not a fan of long, descriptive passages. Even stretched out on a beach towel, with nothing but time and a best-selling novel, I get impatient if the author is long-winded. *If something's happening on a train, just say "on a train". I don't need to read about the leaves on every tree whizzing past the windows!*

In content writing, being verbose is a deadly sin. Readers are busy (and probably not trapped on a beach towel), so if you drone on, they click to something else. That said, succinct doesn't need to be dull.

You can punch up your content without rambling. The secret is to **lean into vivid verbs**.

Replacing weak, over-used verbs with stronger options adds pep and power to your writing. And as an extra benefit, vivid verbs are often more concise and telling.

For example, in the first draft of this chapter, my opening paragraph described trees "speeding past the windows." It was okay. But *"whizzing* past the windows" has a stronger sensation of speed, and *whizzing* is a catchier, more interesting word.

When you're in the first draft phase, don't worry about hunting down the most vivid verbs; just get your thoughts out. But once you start polishing your words, break out the BIG coffee mug and ruminate over those verbs.

Pay particular attention to movement verbs. They're the ones most open to vivid alternatives.

For example: a commonplace movement verb like "walk" tells readers almost nothing. But swap it out for "trudge" and you've created a mood. Try "swagger" and the mood is completely different.

Ask yourself how you want readers to feel. Then use vivid verbs to inspire those feelings and set the scene.

Note: Be more cautious when it comes to verbs for speech, like "said". While the occasional vivid option may be impactful (e.g., "hollered", "whispered", "cried"), if you spread it on too thick, your content becomes melodramatic.

Remember that you're writing online content, not a trashy romance novel!

CHAPTER 42
Pick Stronger Adjectives

"If you need three adjectives to describe something, then you've probably chosen the wrong something."

Roger Rosenblatt, Author, Playwright, Essayist, and Professor

I love adjectives, but only brilliant ones. The rest are rubbish.

Common, over-used adjectives add little to your writing. Think of words like good, great, bad, boring, smart, interesting, fun, sad, happy, big, little. *I'm yawning as I write this.*

These words are vague. They don't do justice to your nouns, and they should be plucked from your sentences like weeds from the garden. "Good" isn't good. "Great" isn't great. "Interesting" isn't interesting. Pick stronger adjectives that have personality.

Weak	Strong
good, great, interesting	brilliant, spectacular, mind-boggling
bad, sad	horrid, devastating, debilitating
big	gargantuan, epic, earth-shattering

So, which adjectives should you keep, and which ones should you kill?

Common adjectives should go. At best, they're wasting space. At worst, they're sucking the life out of your writing. Spicy adjectives, like "gargantuan", may add flavour, so it's fair to keep a few of those.

But don't just swap common adjectives for peppier alternatives. First, ask yourself why each adjective is there. If you're using it to prop up a lame noun, the better choice is to toss away the crutch and find a noun that's capable of doing the heavy lifting. For example:

Dull:	This is a big problem.
Better:	This is a gargantuan problem.
Arguably BEST:	This is a predicament.

"Big" is a bland, over-used adjective. "Gargantuan" is more unique, and clever, but it isn't always going to be appropriate. For instance, it might seem a bit over-the-top in a business report.

"Problem" is the real problem in this sentence. It's dull, and no amount of decoration is going to make it sparkle. That's why the best solution is to replace that flat, lifeless noun with something stronger, like "predicament". This makes the sentence more engaging to readers without bloating the word count or changing the tone.

In general, it's best to remove as many adjectives as possible, and make sure the remaining few are descriptive and purposeful. **Remember that clear outshines clever.**

Try this exercise:

Pull every adjective out of a page of content. Highlight your nouns. Read each sentence aloud. Ask yourself:

Is the meaning of this sentence clear?

Is the noun strong enough?

Would an adjective help?

Play with each sentence. Have fun with them!

CHAPTER 43
Don't Let Adverbs Run Amok

"Adverbs are the tool of the lazy writer."

Mark Twain, Humourist, Journalist, and Novelist

An adverb is a word or set of words that we add to a sentence to describe a verb or an adjective (or sometimes even another adverb). The purpose of the adverb is to expand on *how, when, where,* or *to what extent.*

There's nothing inherently wrong with using adverbs. *See! I just used the adverb "inherently" in a purposeful way.*

The problem is that adverbs aren't always purposeful. Most often, they're just accessories used to dress up lazy writing. For instance, instead of taking the time to find a strong verb or a vibrant descriptor, a lazy writer might toss in "very" and rely on it to do the heavy lifting.

Lazy	Better
very happy	delighted, overjoyed, thrilled, tickled pink
very disappointed	disillusioned, dismayed, frustrated, let down, unsatisfied

very important	crucial, imperative, momentous, valuable

Think of adverbs as the dullest colours in your writing palette. Used properly, they may add a bit of depth or nuance, but they can't create vibrance. An impactful verb works better than a mediocre verb with an adjective tacked on. And a spicy adjective outshines a bland adjective/adverb combination every time.

When it comes to adverbs, less is more:

- Never use them just to make sentences longer or pump up the word count.

- If the adverb doesn't add meaning to the sentence, delete it.

- And don't fall into the habit of using adverbs instead of taking the time to find strong verbs and adjectives.

Don't be a lazy writer. Put effort into your process and choose your words wisely.

CHAPTER 44
Play With Your Transitions

**"Any spot in your structure that makes readers
go 'huh?' is an invitation to quit reading."**

David D. Fryxell, Author and Editor

Transition words are one of those things you notice more by
their absence than their presence. When used properly, they
don't attract your attention. But when they're missing, you
feel the choppiness of the writing. The connection between
one sentence and the next can feel somewhat random, which
reduces the clarity and the impact of your words.

Read each of these options:

1. I love storytelling. Some content writers don't.

2. I love storytelling, but some content writers don't.

There's nothing wrong with the first option, but the second
one flows better. Adding that simple transition (but) smooths
out the change from one line of reasoning to the next.

The good news is that there are more than two hundred
transitional words and phrases to choose from. **When you**

have time, Google "transition words" and download one of the countless charts and infographics available. It's a great resource to have on hand.

In the meantime, here are a few common situations where transitions are called for and some simple words and phrases that I find useful:

Purpose	Options
Additions	And, besides, or
Cause	Because, since
Clarification	In other words, to put it another way
Comparison	In the same way, likewise, similarly
Contrast	But, however, on the other hand, though, yet
Effect	As a result, therefore
Purpose	For this reason, so that
Qualification	Almost, maybe, nearly, never, probably
Time	During, meanwhile, sometimes, soon, later

Now that I've explained why transition words are the BOMB, let me do a quick transition (*ha ha*) into why you shouldn't scatter them like confetti.

Too many transition words and phrases can create bloated paragraphs that have high word counts but low impact. At a certain volume, instead of helping move things forward, they simply create clutter.

As an example, read this paragraph:

> I love storytelling, but some writers don't, and there are legitimate arguments in favour and against. For instance, some studies show that readers are engaged by storytelling. For this

reason, it makes sense to lean into storytelling when creating content. On the other hand, there are studies showing that online readers appreciate writing that gets to the point. Because storytelling is less direct, it may be best to stick to the facts. (Word count: 72)

This paragraph isn't awful, but it meanders more than it needs to. There are so many transitions that they interrupt the narrative instead of helping it flow. There's a sweet spot when it comes to transitions: both too few *and* too many can make your writing choppy and dull.

Going back to the example:

I love storytelling, but some writers don't. While readers find storytelling engaging, they also appreciate writing that gets to the point. Storytelling is less direct, so there are times when it's better to stick to the facts. (Word count: 37)

So much better!

Transition words exist to help connect the dots, but they're not a cure-all. As with everything else, transitions should be used when they're purposeful, but axed if they're just weighing things down. Unnecessary wordiness is a cardinal sin.

CHAPTER 45
Minimize Passive Voice

Passive: Snappy, easy-to-read content is wanted by online readers.

Active: Online readers want snappy, easy-to-read content.

Passive: Attention is grabbed quickly by active voice.

Active: Active voice grabs attention quickly.

Can you feel the difference?

Passive voice isn't wrong. It's just a style choice and sometimes it's appropriate. But too much passive voice sucks the energy out of your writing and makes it harder to read. Active voice has more pizzazz. It gets to the point, and it sounds less pretentious.

When you write in active voice, you use a clear subject + verb + object pattern that's easy to follow. Writing in passive voice scrambles the pattern. In passive voice, the subject is acted on by the verb and the sentence becomes more complicated.

When I was in high school, there was a common cheer at football games. It went like this:

Cheerleaders holler out:	"What do we want?"
Fans bellow back:	"VICTORY!"
Cheerleaders scream again:	"When do we want it?"
Fans go crazy:	"NOW!"

This silly sequence helps me remember the energy and essence of an active voice sentence: *We want victory now!*

Subject = we

Verb = want

Object = victory

In passive voice, this turns into: Victory is wanted now by us. *Even the peppiest cheerleader is going to struggle with that one.*

On the page, passive voice can be hard to spot, especially when editing your own writing. Eyes get lazy, which is why the cure for passive voice overload is to read aloud.

Don't rush. Listen carefully. If your voice sounds monotone or robotic, that's a giveaway that you're pushing through a heavy load of passive voice.

Wherever possible, switch from passive voice to active voice. Keep the focus on the subject and don't overcomplicate your sentence structure. Just this one tweak can make an astounding improvement in a piece of writing.

Remember: **Online readers want snappy, easy-to-read content. Active voice grabs attention quickly!**

CHAPTER 46
Honour Your Primary Tense

Before was was was, it was is.

How's that for a mind-boggling sentence?!?

The English language has more than a dozen tenses and a gazillion rules about how to use them. It's madness. That said, the basic concept of tense is simple. It's how you assign something to the past, the present, or the future.

As a rule of thumb, it's best to pick a primary tense and stick with it. Only switch tenses if you need to highlight something from a different time. For example, here's an excerpt from a piece I wrote on the power of using stories in non-fiction writing:

I believe in the power of storytelling. As my grandma used to say, "Folks love a good yarn."

I wrote this in present tense, but dear old grandma has been dead for years, so I put her in the past—where she belongs.

I prefer present tense when I'm writing on a popular topic and doling out timely facts, ideas, and opinions. But if the content is more academic or technical, I might choose past tense, especially if there are references to things from the past, like completed studies or findings.

Here are a few tips to help master tense control:

- **Listen to your inner voice.** Mine speaks to me in present tense, so when I'm writing, that feels natural to me. Whenever possible, lean into what comes naturally. It's easier and you won't make as many mistakes. *Trust me. When you choose a less comfortable tense, that devilish inner voice may jump in here and there, even without your consent.*

- **Read out loud—like you're talking to someone.** If your writing is in present tense, it should sound like you're telling your imaginary friend about something as it happens. If you're in past tense, it should sound like you're explaining something that happened a while ago.

- **Find a trustworthy reader.** Tense control comes easier to some writers than to others. If you know this isn't your thing, there's no shame in asking for help. Ideally, try to find a real person instead of an online grammar checker, especially for a longer piece of writing. Apps and algorithms have their limitations. While they're useful for finding spelling mistakes and minor punctuation problems, their advice on complicated things like tense, word choice, and style, is less reliable.

Long term, my advice is to read. READ A LOT. Consciously focus on how other writers use tense. In particular, take note of the interesting ways experienced writers weave secondary tenses into their primary choice.

Copy what you like. Disregard the rest.

CHAPTER 47
Control Your Commas

Take a deep breath before reading this.

Giant sentences with no commas only work if your audience is entirely composed of Olympic-calibre swimmers who are both mentally and physically equipped to go extraordinarily long periods of time without feeling the need to inhale.

Pause here to catch your breath.

On the other hand, too many commas, even when used properly, make readers stop, start, and stop again, over and over, producing an effect akin to having the hiccups.

If you're actually hiccupping, pause again and hold your breath.

Where you put commas in a sentence is mostly common sense. Just think about where you would normally pause or change gears, then insert commas into those spots.

That said, if you're drowning in wildly long sentences, overloading them with commas isn't going to save you. That's an editing situation. You need to axe unnecessary words and break things down into shorter, clearer sentences.

And remember when I said comma usage was mostly about common sense? *(It was about 50 words ago)*. Well, that's true. But it's also about tradition.

Enter the unending debate about the Oxford comma...

Traditionally, the Oxford comma, sometimes called the serial comma, is placed before the last item on a list. In British writing, the Oxford comma is still standard. But American writers, especially journalists, prefer to skip it.

With an Oxford comma:	I love poetry, fiction, and non-fiction.
Without an Oxford comma:	I love poetry, fiction and non-fiction.

So, who's right? The persnickety Europeans? Or the care-free Americans?

The Americans will argue that it's a wanton waste of space, and in some formats, like social media posts, they may have a point. When your available character count is finite, the two characters you're sacrificing for the Oxford comma and subsequent spacing might be used for more critical things— like a poopy face emoji or two explanation points. *Yes, that was sarcasm. No one needs a poopy face emoji or doubled exclamation points.*

I embrace the Oxford comma. It's orderly and efficient. That final comma works like a cutlery drawer, effectively ensuring that each item has a designated home.

Neat and tidy:	knives, forks, and spoons
Less neat and tidy:	knives, forks and spoons

Without that final comma, I'm unsure about the status of those forks and spoons. Are they separate? Or are they mixed and mingled together while the knives live alone? *Both the uncertainty and the thought of them mingling bother me.*

In my ideal world, we all agree to use the Oxford comma. That said, if it's not your thing, that's fine, so long as you're consistent.

I worry about the state of your kitchen drawers, but I respect your preferences.

CHAPTER 48
Use Bullet Points Properly

Giant walls of text can be intimidating. Bullet points are a great tool for tearing down some of those walls and helping readers grab important information quickly.

Used properly, bulleted lists can:

- Highlight specifics

- Capture the attention of readers

- Improve the readability of your content

Note that this is an example of how to use a bulleted list properly. I'm writing about bullet points, so it's on-topic, and I've used parallel form for readability.

Wondering what parallel form is?

Parallel form is about consistently using the same part of speech. In the list I just gave you, "highlight", "capture", and "improve" are all verbs. This makes it easy to read. If you abandon parallel form, readability dissolves.

Here's what my list might look like without applying the principle of parallel form:

Used properly, bulleted lists can:

- Shine a light on highpoints

- Readers will pay more attention

- Content becomes more readable

See the problem?

Only the first bullet point completes the lead-in ("bulleted lists can ___"). Worse yet, the three options are no longer grammatically consistent. One starts with a verb but the other two start with nouns, and two use present tense, while one is written in future tense.

Even if readers don't know exactly what's wrong with the structure of those bullet points, they may have an icky feeling when they're reading. And you don't want that icky feeling to take root because it inspires them to leave the page.

Here are a few tips to ensure that your bulleted lists are a turn-on and not a turn-off.

- Worship parallel form. Don't create a hodgepodge of verb and noun beginnings.

- Make sure each statement properly completes the lead-in.

- If you use periods, use them on each statement, and only use them if you're creating complete sentences.

Don't be afraid of bullet points. They can be brilliant! But remember that a sturdy house relies on walls for substance and stability. It's fine to open up the floorplan, but be strategic about which paragraphs you dismantle - and why.

CHAPTER 49
Axe the Air Quotes

Air quotes are an American invention.

In a face-to-face conversation, when someone raises two fingers up and down on either side of their head like bunny ears, they're indicating that their words shouldn't be taken verbatim. Writers achieve the same effect by placing quotation marks around a word or phrase purely to draw attention to it.

Whether talking or writing, air quotes are a no-no. **They're almost always meanness disguised as humour.** Most often, they're used to dismiss an idea, a person, or a group of people, which is *not* cool!

For example, if you put air quotes around the word "expert", readers know what you're *really* saying about that individual's expertise. And it's not nice.

If you take argument with something or someone, do it directly. Delete the air quotes and use grown-up words and intelligent arguments to express yourself.

For instance, if you want to diminish the power of an expert opinion, a simple solution is to present other viewpoints:

"While some experts believe _____, there are others who say _____."

As a writer, your words and your punctuation choices have power. **Always err on the side of respectful discourse.**

CHAPTER 50
Don't Scream at People

NO ONE LIKES TO BE SHOUTED AT!

The exclusive use of capital letters is the written equivalent to shouting. It can come across as aggressive and rude, so it's generally best to avoid hitting the caps lock key. Be respectful and use your indoor voice.

That said, monotone is boring. In real life, voices go up and down. We speak louder when we want to emphasize something, and people DO pay more attention to that loudness. Sprinkling a few capitalized words here and there can be an effective trick to capture attention and add a bit of exuberance. But you need to sprinkle, not pour.

Here are some do's and don'ts when comes to CAPS:

Do: Capitalize a few KEY WORDS to add emphasis.

Don't: CAPITALIZE AN ENTIRE SENTENCE, ESPECIALLY A LONG ONE, BECAUSE IT'S OVERWHELMING.

Do: Use CAPS to express positive feelings, like happiness, love, and excitement. For example, "LOVE THIS!" is cute.

Don't: Use CAPS to express strong negative feelings, like anger. For example, "HATE THIS!" feels threatening, bordering on homicidal.

Do: Use CAPS to insert some personality into informal content formats, like social media posts.

Don't: Use CAPS in formal communications, like proposals, reports, or white papers. Prescribed formats like these call for a stately tone and controlled emotions. No screaming. And avoid CAPS in direct marketing messages. "Buy Now" is polite. "BUY NOW" is aggressive and spammy.

Think of CAPS as content decorations. Great for when you want to add a splash of colour but a little goes a LONG way!

CHAPTER 51
Check Your Spelling

Spelling mistakes draw attention like spaghetti stains on a white shirt. Once you see them, you can't unsee them.

They lower the authority of your writing because they imply carelessness. Too many misspelled words can diminish the perceived value of your content, even if your message is important and your facts are accurate. *Interestingly, "misspelled" is a commonly misspelled word. Folks skip the second "s" and end up with "mispelled".*

In a first draft, the occasional typo may be unavoidable, so spellchecking is an important part of the editing process. Don't rush it, even if your timeline is tight, because that's how a second "s" gets lost.

Automatic spellcheckers can be helpful, but they're also quirky, and sometimes their corrections make matters worse. My pet peeve is when they pressure me to swap out British/Canadian spellings for American versions. *It's "favourite", not "favorite", damn it!*

I believe in personal vigilance when it comes to spelling. Examine each sentence with a hawklike gaze. And if you're not a strong speller, or if the piece is especially long and complex, find someone to jump in and take a second peek. *Four eyeballs are better than two!*

CHAPTER 52
Watch Your Tone

**"Watch your tone, saucy-pants!
Remember who you're talking to."**

My Grandma

My grandma had a zero tolerance policy when it came to anything she deemed saucy. On a few occasions, when I felt wrongly accused, I would complain to my mother. But regardless of my arguments and excuses, Mom's answer was always the same. She would give me the evil eye and declare, "If Grandma feels like you were saucy, you were saucy."

My mother was right because tone isn't just about the words you use. It's about how you use them and how they make people feel.

In writing, tone is the *vibe* you send out to readers. It's the cumulative effect of everything from word choice to sentence structure and punctuation. Tone is also impacted by non-text elements, like images, videos, emojis, and gifs.

Minor changes can make a big difference in tone. For example:

Polite and professional:	Thank you for visiting.
Friendlier and less formal:	Thanks for visiting.
More enthusiastic:	Thanks so much for visiting!
Casual and fun:	Thank YOU for visiting!

Because everything on the page contributes to tone, your challenge is to be intentional about your choices. And to be intentional, you need to know from the beginning what tone you're going for.

As a content writer, you're probably aiming for a tone that falls into one of these buckets:

- **Knowledgeable and Professional**

   Example: A white paper or in-depth guide written for a professional audience

- **Friendly and Informative**

   Example: A how-to article aimed at a general audience

- **Empowering and Uplifting**

   Example: Website content for a motivational brand, like a weight loss program

You want to use a writing style, language, and expressions that are familiar to your audience and align with the purpose of your piece.

Let's say you're creating a white paper and you want readers to *feel* how **knowledgeable and professional** you are. If that's the tone you're going for:

- It's best to use formal language (e.g., "thank you" rather than "thanks".)

- It's okay to use technical words that are well-known to your audience, so long as you don't overdo it and end up in a pit of jargon.

- You-and-I language might work but it's not essential because warmth isn't a key tonal element for this type of writing.

- Skip cutesy things like cartoon images, gifs, and jokes. It can diminish your authority. *So, don't lead with a quote from your grandma.*

If you're going for **friendly and informative:**

- Lighten the language. Replace longer words with shorter, more common options. Avoid jargon and insider terms.

- Use you-and-I language, if possible.

- Add storytelling elements, like analogies and personal narratives, to reinforce that friendly vibe.

- Don't go overboard, but be open to options like adding emojis, fun quotes, and colourful images. *That quote from Grandma may work!*

- Add a dollop of humour, so long as it's sensitive and respectful to your audience.

To shift into **empowering and uplifting:**

- Language is important. Choose powerful, affirmative words and statements (e.g., "You can do it!" and "You've got this!").

- You-and-I language is a must. You want to put readers into the action and inspire them.

- Don't add exclamation points everywhere. They can come across as aggressive instead of motivational.

- Depending on the topic, you can go light, medium, or heavy, on elements like humour, emojis, gifs, and images.

Writing Exercise:

Look at something you've already written. Ask yourself what the tone is. Now, experiment with punctuation, sentence structure, and word choice. See if you can create a version of that piece that fits into each of the three tone buckets.

If you're not sure you've nailed it, find a grandma. They're brutally honest.

CHAPTER 53
Don't Dress Up Opinions as Facts

**"Everyone is entitled to his own opinion,
but not his own facts."**

Daniel Patrick Moynihan,
American Politician, Sociologist, and Diplomat

Unsupported Opinion:	I think raw tomatoes are yucky.
Supported Opinion:	I think raw tomatoes are yucky because they're full of slimy sacs of seeds.
Opinion dressed up as fact:	Raw tomatoes are yucky. People dislike the slimy sacs of seeds.

There's nothing wrong with expressing an opinion. It can add personality to your writing, and if you're a subject matter expert, your opinion may be exactly what people are looking for. That said, **opinions are not facts and presenting them as facts is a no-no**.

It's important to make sure readers clearly understand when you're sharing a viewpoint versus an objective truth. The simplest way to do this is to precede your opinion with a clarifying statement, like "I think", "I believe", or "In my opinion".

Example: I think raw tomatoes are yucky.

If the subject of debate is something as benign as the taste of a tomato, or if your only goal is to make your opinion public, this approach is fine. But if you're trying to persuade readers to see things your way, you should add a supporting argument. The strongest supporting facts are usually data and statistics, but even an objective observation can do the trick.

Example: I think raw tomatoes are yucky because they're full of slimy sacs of seeds.

"Slimy" isn't the most objective descriptor because it strongly implies yuckiness. But it's not inaccurate, just gross.

Choosing persuasive words is fine, but beware the risk of stretching too far, to suit your argument. There's a slippery slope between persuasion and exaggeration. And exaggeration slides easily into lying:

Example: Raw tomatoes are yucky. People dislike the slimy sacs of seeds.

The slimy sacs of seeds are a fact, but the word "people" conjures up the idea of *everyone*. And that's one step too far down that slippery slope.

As an alternative, "some people" would be less of a stretch since it's safe to assume that some people like or dislike almost anything you can think of. "People may dislike" would also be a better choice because it's less definitive.

When it comes to transparency and separating fact from opinion, subtle differences matter. During the editing process, keep your eyes open for both unsupported opinions and opinions dressed up as facts. It's surprising how easily they can slip into a rough draft, especially when you're writing about something you feel strongly about.

Like raw tomatoes.

I think they're yucky.

CHAPTER 54
Add Impactful Quotes

**"A very wise quote is a spectacular waterfall.
When you see it, you feel its power!"**

Mehmet Murat Ildan, Playwright, Novelist, and Thinker

There's no shame in sharing the words of others. In fact, it's a brilliant way to engage readers and strengthen whatever point you're trying to make. For example, I opened this chapter with this quote by Mehmet Murat Ildan, because he described the glory of a wise quote so beautifully.

Quotes are a wonderful writing accessory. That said, like all accessories, they are most effective when used strategically and in moderation. Here are a few situations where quotes can be useful:

- If you're struggling to find an engaging opener, a quote (like Mehmet's) can pique interest and pull readers in.

- When you want to add authority to your opinion, a supportive quote does the job beautifully. *As Argentine novelist, Julio Cortazar, tells us, "In quoting others, we cite ourselves".*

- Visually, quotes create welcome breaks in longer pieces of content.

Because quotes are innately shareable, they also tempt readers to share your content with others. In this way, they can help you connect with a larger audience.

For the most part, picking the right quote is simple. You just hunt around until you find one that tickles your fancy. That said, here are a few considerations:

- **Be conscious of WHO is making the quote**. For example, I once quoted car maker Henry Ford in an article about the value of workplace diversity and was subsequently lambasted in the comments section, for good reason. Turns out he was known for being racist and anti-Semitic.

- **Be inclusive**. It's easy to end up quoting mostly men, and more specifically, white men. Their words are everywhere. But the world is full of diverse, beautiful voices, equally worthy of being heard. Use your power as a writer to showcase diversity.

- **Don't be trite.** Avoid inane quotes that you might imagine scrawled in a romantic font on a toss cushion or piece of wall art. Say something worth saying.

Perhaps most importantly, always give credit where credit is due. Respect the creator of the words! Quotes are good. Plagiarism is bad.

CHAPTER 55
Never Resort to Fluff-and-Filler

Word count isn't everything, but it's SOMETHING, and sometimes it's important.

For instance, if your headline promises readers a deep dive into something, your word count must be significant enough to fulfill that promise. And if a client pays you to create 3,000 words, you definitely need to produce 3,000 words.

Most often, when you find yourself struggling to meet word count expectations, the problem stems from a lack of planning. By planning, I mean:

- Research your topic until you understand it thoroughly.

- Take the time to create an outline that factors in the required length.

When you know what you're talking about (research) and you've got a solid plan of attack (outline), the word count usually works out. You may find yourself needing to expand or retract a bit, but you'll probably land in the right ballpark.

If you're nowhere near the right ballpark, you've got two options: go back to the planning stage or adjust your word count expectations. DO NOT succumb to the temptation of stretching things with fluff-and-filler. It's a sign of lazy writing. Worse yet, it buries your valuable insights under an avalanche of word litter.

The most common fluff-and-filler trick is to stuff unnecessary words into sentences and paragraphs. For example, a clear statement like "research is important" (Word count 3) might become a monstrosity, like:

> "The point must be made that research is an integral and important element in the planning process that should not be disregarded or minimized." (Word count: 24).

Just writing that second sentence made my eyes roll to the back of my head, and I sighed in dismay.

Other fluff-and-filler tactics include things like adding vaguely related content, providing multiple examples when one is good enough, and repeating the same argument more than once. You can get away with a little of this nonsense. But at some point, your sentences become so cumbersome, and your content so discombobulated, that readers lose interest.

If you're so close to the ideal word count that you can taste it, there are a few harmless ways to inch across the finish line, like adding a quote, or a few statistics, or even a brief anecdote (if it fits with the tone). But if you're off target by 500+ words, my advice is to go back to the drawing board.

You may find additional information worth sharing or you may not. And if that's the case, so be it. **NEVER sacrifice quality for quantity.**

CHAPTER 56
Do a Respect Check

"Respect begins with this attitude: I acknowledge that you are a creature of extreme worth."

Gary Chapman, Author and Radio Talk Show Host

Your readers are not a demographic, or a market segment, or a search engine. They are living, breathing people who could have chosen a zillion other things to read, but they chose *your* content.

They are willingly giving you their time and their attention. These are incredibly valuable gifts. As a writer, you demonstrate appreciation and respect for readers when you:

- Provide valuable information and insights.

- Take time to polish your words so that reading is a pleasure, not a chore.

- Demonstrate integrity, which means:

    o Don't disguise promotional writing as something else.

o   Don't plagiarize.

o   Don't promise an "ultimate guide" and deliver a few hundred words of general information.

Most importantly, never talk down to your readers. You can demonstrate authority and expertise without climbing onto a podium.

Before you publish any piece of writing, do a quick RESPECT CHECK: Imagine that you're talking to someone you know and respect. If you catch a hint of arrogance in the tone of your words, keep editing!

CHAPTER 57
Embrace Inclusive Language

**"No matter what anybody tells you, words
and ideas can change the world."**

John Keating, Character in the film *Dead Poet's Society*

Inclusive language isn't about political correctness or about using the right words for a particular demographic. It's about respect. It's about recognizing the power of your words and consciously choosing language that welcomes and values every reader.

When it comes to inclusive language, here are a few guidelines:

- Avoid defining people based on a single part of their identity. For example, rather than refer to someone as disabled, say "person with a disability".

- Avoid irrelevant descriptions of appearance. Unless it's pertinent to the topic, don't add details about someone's age, height, hair colour, clothing, or level of attractiveness.

- Avoid terms that contribute to stigmas around disability or mental illness. Never use offensive words like crazy, dumb, psycho, or stupid.

- Unless you know someone's pronouns, use they/them rather than he/his or she/hers. And *yes*, it's grammatically correct to use they/them as a singular pronoun.

- Demonstrate respect for the universe of gender identities. Simple things, like saying "different" sex instead of "opposite" sex, and they instead of he/she are important ways to move beyond adherence to the male/female binary.

- Consciously replace gendered words and phrases with gender neutral alternatives. So much of our language is gendered that we drop such terms into our writing without even noticing. But in most cases, there are gender neutral options that are just as commonplace and easy to use. For example:

  o Mother/father => parent

  o Girlfriend/boyfriend => partner

  o Wife/husband => partner or spouse

  o Ladies and gentlemen => distinguished guests

  o Hi guys => Hi folks or Hi everyone

Language is constantly evolving. As a writer, it's part of your job to be vigilant about the words you choose. Watch for and delete terms that have become antiquated, and embrace positive, inclusive words that welcome readers and build trust.

CHAPTER 58
Read With Your Ears

"Reading aloud is the only way to know if a sentence really works, without clunks or cul-de-sac clauses."

Anna Quindlan, Author, Journalist, and Opinion Columnist

When you're writing, your brain is busily sorting through ideas, making choices, and plotting all the little twists and turns from your first sentence to your last. This familiarity can be a problem because by the time you proofread your own work, your brain may be on autopilot. It already knows where you're going, so it's not looking at the scenery anymore.

That's why you need to read aloud. When you toss your words into the universe and let them ricochet back, everything sounds new and different. Your brain responds by turning off autopilot and paying more attention.

Reading aloud helps you notice small things, like misspelled words and punctuation errors, but it also helps you see bigger issues. For instance:

- **Weak arguments, incomplete points, and leaps of logic** stand out more clearly when your brain isn't unconsciously filling things in for you.

- **Rambling sentences, over-wrought descriptions, and weak word choices** suddenly pop into view.

- **Flow problems** become more obvious because your tongue twists when it hits a bump. *It's the difference between looking at the lyrics of a song versus trying to sing it.*

The moment you commit to reading everything aloud, your writing will improve. Guaranteed!

It may feel painful sometimes because reading aloud almost always leads to more edits. But it's still the best way to *really* see (and hear) how well you're playing with words.

CHAPTER 59
Ask Yourself the Three Big Questions

The process of editing commonly focuses on the words and how you've placed them on the page, which is important stuff, no doubt about it. But demonstrating your grammatical prowess isn't the end game.

Words are the tools of your trade but **communicating is your purpose**. So, before you publish anything, it's important to back up and look at the big picture one last time. Go beyond the words and ponder your message and your tone.

Ask yourself the three BIG questions:

- Is it accurate?

- Is it helpful?

- Is the tone respectful?

If the answer to any one of these questions is less than an enthusiastic, "Hell, yes!", you're not finished!

CHAPTER 60
Enjoy Your Tea and Cookies

"Perfectionism is the voice of the oppressor."

Anne Lamott, Novelist, Non-fiction Writer,
and Writing Teacher

You've written and rewritten. Edited, and edited, and edited again. Your spelling is perfection, and your punctuation would make an English teacher weep with joy. Your points have been made, your arguments are sewn up tight, and the whole thing flows like a springtime river.

So, the question is, are you done? And the answer is—maybe.

That critical voice inside your head may want to tweak the ending one more time or hunt down a few renegade adverbs, and if you've still got some gas left in the tank, go for it! But truthfully, that critical voice will never be 100% appeased. So, at some point, you must simply accept that you've given it your all—and stop.

Sometimes, that's what "done" feels like. More surrender than triumph.

You've worked hard and you're likely tired, which is why I recommend putting on the kettle. This is the time to be kind to yourself.

Steep a strong cup of tea and put a few cookies on a pretty plate. *I'm a big fan of shortbreads in these situations, but chocolate chip will work.*

Sip your tea and enjoy your cookies. Pat yourself on the back. Smile. Accept that you've done your best and that your best is enough. You're done.

PART 5
Capture Attention and Hold It

People read differently online than they do in print. In fact, most of the time, they don't read at all. They just scan.[3]

Online readers are impatient, but they're also purposeful! If they quickly recognize the value of your content, they're inclined to slow down and spend a bit more time on the page. In fact, you may even coax them into reading.

So, the challenge is not just to write spectacular content; it's also to use language and word placement strategically. You need to hook them and pull them in, lickety-split, before their attention falters.

In this section, I'm going to talk about how to create powerful headlines and openers, skim-able content, and strong endings.

---

[3] Neilson Norman Group, How People Read Online: New and Old Findings, April 2020, https://www.nngroup.com/articles/how-people-read-online, (accessed 7 October, 2021).

CHAPTER 61
Hook Them with Your Headline

"You have to get a great headline to attract attention. It's about the lure—not the rod."

Michael Hyatt, Author, Podcaster, Speaker, and Entrepreneur

Your headline is the first point of contact with potential readers. Its purpose is to capture their attention and inspire them to click. And if you fail, your words of wisdom won't be read, so crafting a solid headline is important.

The practicalities of headline writing are relatively simple. Stay under 70 characters (so your title doesn't get cut off in search engine results) and use your keyword or keyword phrase in the headline. For example, if your topic is about content writing:

- o "How to Craft Magical Words that Jump Off the Page" is creative but vague.

- o "How to Write Content that Jumps Off the Page" gives both search engines and real people more context. *There are undoubtedly more folks searching for ways to "write content" than ways to "craft magical words". Just saying.*

Beyond the practical, there are several Golden Rules when it comes to headlines:

- **Be clear and specific about the value of your content.** Tell folks exactly what you're going to give them. For example:

  o "How to Write Content that Jumps Off the Page" is solid, but

  o "6 Easy Ways to Write Content that Jumps Off the Page" is arguably better because it promises six concrete takeaways.

- **Be truthful.** If you promise readers "6 Easy Ways" to do something, make sure that's what you give them. And establish the relevance of the headline in your first paragraph. *If your "6 Easy Ways" article starts with a rambling story about how you became a content writer, folks will feel duped, and they'll leave.*

- **Be concise.** If you can replace multiple words with one word and not lose meaning or impact, do it. For instance:

  o "6 Easy Ways to Write Content that Jumps Off the Page" is nice, but

  o "6 Easy Ways to Write Content that Pops" has the same vibe and takes up less space.

- **Use a HOT word, if possible.** In the headline I just gave you, "Pops" is the hot word. It adds spice and interest. That said, when it comes to spices, moderation is key. Too many can spark eyerolls instead of excitement.

Ultimately, you want to create a catchy headline that leads your ideal readers to content that gives them exactly what they're looking for.

Your headline is a first impression—make it a good one!

CHAPTER 62
Own the First 10 Seconds

10 seconds. That's how long you have. If you can't capture someone's attention in those first ten seconds, they click away.

30 seconds. That's how long you need to hold their attention so that they settle down and give your writing a chance. If you can keep their eyeballs on the page for 30 seconds, research shows that readers become less distracted. They may even stay engaged for a few minutes, which is an eternity in the online world.

Herein lies the problem. Your topic is probably important and impactful. It may be exactly what they're looking for. But that doesn't make it instantly fascinating.

So how do you meet the demand for immediate gratification?

You hit them with your best shot first.

Fiction writers may have the luxury of setting the scene and slowly building tension, but you don't. Your reader probably isn't stretched out on their sofa with a cup of tea or lounging on the beach. More likely, they're hunched forward, eyes intensely staring at a screen, fingers itching to click or scroll.

So, you don't have time to woo them or cajole them. You've got to COMMAND their attention.

Notice how I started this chapter. I didn't ramble on about the research or the underlying principles of engagement. I hit you with a two-word sentence that sparked curiosity: 10 seconds.

The moment you read that sentence, your subconscious demanded to know, "*What happens in 10 seconds?*"

After the briefest explanation possible, I hit you with another curious number to keep pulling you forward: 30 seconds.

Depending on how fast you read, it took somewhere between 20 and 30 seconds for you to get through those first paragraphs. Hopefully, that was enough time for your impatience to subside and your interest in the content to deepen.

Here are some solid starters that can buy a few seconds of attention:

- Quotes

- Statistics

- Testimonials

- Jokes

- Questions to the reader

Think short. Fast. Impactful.

And remember that online content is intensely visual. Don't be afraid to use **bold letters,** *italics,* CAPITALS, <u>underlined words,</u> or exclamation points!

In fact, maybe you should go hog wild with ***<u>A BOLD, CAPITALIZED, UNDERLINED, ITALICIZED, SENTENCE CAPPED OFF WITH MULTIPLE EXPLANATION POINTS!!!!</u>***

Just kidding. That's obnoxious. *But you get my point. It's okay to be a bit dramatic in your opener.*

Go big and hit hard.

CHAPTER 63
Be Skim-Able

Let's say you've written 3,000+ words of brilliance. *Congrats!*

You're giving folks a ton of in-depth, meaty knowledge, which is great. But you're also demanding a lot from them. First, you're asking them to choose your content above all the other options. Then, you're expecting them to give you at least ten minutes of their undivided attention, because 3,000+ words are a lot to process.

It's a BIG ask.

People are busy and impatient. Most readers won't jump into a long-form article without skimming over it first. So, to make sure your content beats out the competition and provides value to readers, you need to **make sure it's skim-able.**

Here are a few simple ways to improve your skim-ability:

- **Don't crowd the page.** White space is important. It makes it easy for readers to scan an article and find bits of content that are of particular interest.

- **Choose a clear, easy font and a decent font size.** I once opened a three-page article written entirely in a calligraphy-style font. Then I closed it. The end.

- **Create meaningful headlines and sub-headings.** Skimmers read these first, so make sure they convey valuable information and spark interest in exploring those smaller words underneath.

For instance, if you're writing about a process, swap generic sub-headings like "Step One", "Step Two", and so on, for more descriptive options. The first step might become something like:

o   How to Prepare
o   Setting the Stage for Success
o   Before You Begin

- **Keep paragraphs short**

Giant chunks of writing are intimidating and make pages look crowded. Whenever possible, create shorter paragraphs that are easy to digest and accommodate white space. I recommend varying your paragraph lengths, with some as short as a single sentence, and the majority no more than three sentences.

- **Use bullet points and numbered lists**

Bullet points are visually appealing to skimmers. Where you can break a complicated idea or process into simple, actionable steps, do so.

- **Add visuals**

  Illustrations and photos attract the eye. When you present some data and key points in visual formats, like images and infographics, you increase the chance of readers honing in on that information.

By making your content skim-able, you may help turn mildly interested skimmers into full-fledged readers. Worst case scenario, they remain skimmers, but are still able to grab a few morsels of helpful knowledge. Either way, you've communicated, so it's a win!

CHAPTER 64
Nail the Dismount

I remember watching an amazing gymnast perform on a beam at the Olympics. She was mesmerizing. Then she stumbled on the dismount and the entire audience sighed in disappointment.

Half an hour later, when commentators reviewed the event, she was mentioned only once, in a cursory comment about her failure to nail the dismount. And as I write this chapter, I'm struggling—and failing—to recall her name.

Lesson learned: Endings are important!

From a cognitive perspective, we remember beginnings and endings more than middles. It's just how humans are. So, in terms of making an impression on readers, your first paragraph and your last paragraph are generally more important than everything in between. Sad but true.

You can create the meatiest, most powerful middle ever written, but if the ending is dull, most of that power just trickles away.

So, how do you make those final sentences memorable and satisfying?

The key is to **focus on your purpose**. Ask yourself what the most important takeaway is. If readers only remember *one* thing, what do you want it to be?

- If you want them to **remember a particular point**, repeat it in your final paragraph.

- If your purpose is to help them **understand a process**, summarize the steps.

- If your goal is to **motivate readers to do something**, end with a call to action.

- If you want them to **care more deeply, or think more** about your topic, try leaving them with an inspiring quote or a thought-provoking question.

- If your ambition is to **make them feel capable and confident**, be direct and end with a "You've got this" sort of statement.

Your ending doesn't need to have the snap-crackle-pop of your first paragraph, but it does require substance. Readers should feel as though they're leaving with something more than they started with.

When I'm stuck on the ending (and I am frequently stuck on the ending), I find it helpful to put the whole thing away for a day. Sometimes, after a few hours of not obsessing, things seem clearer.

There's no explaining why this works, but it often does.

The important thing is to keep at it. Don't settle for a weak ending.

It may take a bit of time, effort, *and possibly swearing,* but nailing the dismount is essential if you want people to remember your name—and your message!

PART 6
Master the Long Game

In my experience, there's a natural correlation between getting better at something and enjoying it more. So, if you're going to be writing content on more than a casual, now-and-again basis, you want to elevate your game.

Own it. Be the best content writer you can be and take pride in your work. That said, don't obsess, because obsessing seldom ends well.

Life is a glorious adventure, and you don't want to miss out on parts of the fun because you're locked away in a tiny room, staring at a screen, and plucking madly at a keyboard from dawn until dusk.

In this section, I'm going to talk about ways to maximize the quality and quantity of your work, as well as the pleasure you take in it. Because liking what you do counts!

CHAPTER 65
Be Proactive When It Comes to Writer's Block

Question: Where would a content writer *never* want to live?
Answer: A writer's block

Insert corny, knock-knock-joke sort of laughter here.

There's nothing less funny or more frustrating than not being able to squeeze out words of brilliance—especially when you have a looming deadline. And so many things can trigger writer's block:

- You may be pre-occupied by happenings in your personal life, or world events.

- Maybe you're tired or coming down with the flu.

- Or, God forbid, the topic feels dull.

For me, the most common trigger is over-working. When I've been creating content for days on end, there comes a point where my creativity shuts down.

I imagine my creative side as an office space filled with bright, colourful cubicles. *Picture the Disney cartoon version of a call centre.*

Inside each cubicle is an adorable yellow minion. On good days, the little minions whistle while they work. But if I push them too hard—or for too long—they revolt and go on strike.

Once they hit the picket line, berating them will *not* help. In fact, the more I give in to negative feelings like annoyance, or even rage, the worse things get. The managerial relationship between my logical brain and those creative minions cannot be based on bullying and brute force.

That's why I recommend that your first response to writer's block should be to stop writing. While it feels counterproductive, the fastest way to get back on track is usually to press PAUSE.

This is easy to say, but it can be really hard to do.

You want to get the job done. The deadline's getting closer. The clock is ticking louder and louder. Pausing feels like giving up—but it isn't.

Taking your fingers off the keyboard is necessary and smart. Your creative minions need time to relax. Here are a few things I do to help re-energize:

- **Breathe.** I have a meditation cushion in my office, and it gets lots of use. I've never managed to meditate the way *real* meditators do it, with incense and pan flute music. But I still enjoy closing my eyes and taking a few deep breaths. *It's surprising how just a few minutes of focusing on breathing can clear the mind.*

- **Fuel Your Body.** Dehydration + low blood sugar = low concentration and high anxiety. For years, I suffered with the terrible habit of filling up on coffee, skipping breakfast, and crashing midway through the workday. Then I figured out that drinking a full glass of water and eating a healthy snack was an almost instant cure. Now, I keep a water bottle and a bag of almonds on my desk to ward off hangry (hungry/angry) moments. And I switch to herbal teas in the afternoon.

- **Take a Power Nap.** Sometimes breathing, eating, and re-hydrating isn't enough. Your creative minions are exhausted, and you need to put them down for a nap. Twenty to thirty minutes of sleep can make a remarkable improvement in *everything*. There's a soft, super-comfy chair in one corner of my office. It has a small blanket tossed over one side, as though the whole set up is for decoration. But really, this is my secret napping spot. FYI: Some of history's most creative thinkers, including Aristotle and Einstein, were daily nappers.

- **Get Outside and Move Around.** If you're more stressed than tired, swap out downtime for up-time. Sneakers are your friend, so keep them nearby. Going for a run or a brisk walk is one of the best ways to clear your head. Aim for 30 minutes to an hour, but in a pinch, even a 15-minute scurry around the block may help, and it certainly won't hurt.

- **Do a Writing Exercise.** This advice may seem wacky, but sometimes writing about something new and different clears the cobwebs. I have a collection of writing-prompt journals, each filled with questions and scenarios to spark creativity. I'm a fan of writing-prompts. Besides helping with writer's block, they're a fantastic way to improve your overall skills and help refine your voice.

- **Be Creative in a Different Way.** If completing a writing exercise feels overwhelming, try switching to something visual. Draw a picture. Doodle. Get out your fine-tipped markers and dive into the pages of an adult colouring book. Shifting your creativity to a different medium can be remarkably helpful. Other creative options include things like knitting, crocheting, origami, or even putting together jigsaw puzzles. Ultimately, these activities work because they distract you while simultaneously keeping your creative juices flowing.

- **Read a Book.** The catch here is that it must be a *good* book—something well written. I keep an old, dog-eared copy of *To Kill a Mockingbird* in my office. When I feel an impending block, I pause and read a few pages. Any of the pages. Because Harper Lee was brilliant and her words are perfection. I don't know why this works. Maybe a little bit of her genius temporarily rubs off on me. Or maybe she pulls me into the storyline so fast and so far that I let go of whatever stressor is causing the problem.

- **Call a Friend.** Talking to someone about your topic is a great way to stir the embers and unearth new ideas and perspectives. And let's be honest, sometimes you just need to vent. A good friend can empathize with your frustration and offer reassurance that the situation is only temporary.

Note: Don't be the person who only calls when they have a problem or want to talk about themselves. No one likes THAT person. Make sure you're equally available when your friend needs to be the centre of attention.

- **Change Locations.** My workspace is beautiful and functional, and I absolutely love it, but sometimes a change is as good as a cure. Taking your laptop to a coffee shop can be helpful. *And even if it doesn't work, you're still enjoying cappuccino and pastries.*

  I'm also a fan of the library because being surrounded by books makes me feel more writer-ly. In a pinch, even moving to a new room can help. *But chances are you won't get cappuccino and pastries, so this should be a last resort.*

These things work for me, but that doesn't mean they'll work for you. Not everybody grooves on naps, or adult colouring books, or *To Kill a Mockingbird*.

The most important thing isn't *what* you do while you're pressing pause—it's that you give yourself permission to pause, and you listen to your mind and body. They will tell you what you need.

If you're hungry, eat. If you're tired, rest. Breathe deep. Get fresh air. Do something interesting. Give your mind and body a break.

Remember that writer's block is *not* a permanent condition. It will pass.

CHAPTER 66
Focus on Simplifying the Complicated

"The ability to simplify means to eliminate the unnecessary so that the necessary may speak."

Hans Hofmann, Abstract Expressionist Artist

I hate the expression "dumbing down". It implies that there's something inferior about communicating in plain language that a general audience can understand. The truth is the exact opposite.

Anyone with a decent education and a thesaurus can spew a bunch of gobbledygook onto a page. But it requires intelligence, creativity, and serious writing skills to create clear, precise content, and the more complex the topic is, the greater that challenge becomes.

Honing your ability to simplify the complicated takes time, but it's well worth the investment. Because once you've mastered this art, you can write effectively about any subject and connect with any audience.

How amazing is that?!

When it comes to online content, things like page layout, images, and videos can help (or hinder) the effectiveness of your communication, but it's still mostly about the writing.

Trust me. A snazzy infographic won't save the day if the surrounding text is a red-hot mess. Folks will still click away and continue their search for words that are easier to read.

So how do you boil things down and make complicated concepts easier to understand?

It's not difficult, but it does require deliberate, conscious choices. I've covered these things in earlier chapters, but it never hurts to summarize, so here goes:

- **Never use a long, technical term or bit of insider jargon if there's a short, common word that can do the trick.** *I know I used the word "gobbledygook" in my second paragraph, but I stand by that decision. It's a mouthful but it has a HUGE personality!*

- **Replace passive voice with active voice whenever possible.** Active voice usually requires fewer words and is easier for readers to understand. Example:

  Passive Voice: Multiple programs and services are managed by our organization. (9 words)

  Active Voice: Our organization manages multiple programs and services. (7 words)

- **Use sub-headings.** Think of them as breadcrumbs, gently leading your readers through a dense forest.

- **Keep your paragraphs short.** Remember that some readers are likely using a tablet or phone. Scrolling down those tiny screens can make a long paragraph seem even more onerous.

- **Use images and videos strategically.** A well-chosen visual can help put things in context and reduce the need for detailed explanations. As the familiar adage tells us, sometimes a picture is worth a thousand words.

- **Lean into anecdotes, analogies, and examples.** Storytelling is a great way to pull abstract concepts into the real world. And frankly, writing is more interesting when you add a story element.

- **If someone said it better, let them.** Quotes can be a great way to get the job done quickly. For example, I introduced this section with Hans Hofmann's explanation of what simplifying means. *Why ramble on for a paragraph or more when good old Hans already explained it perfectly?*

- **Go over everything with a fine-tooth comb.** While I know I'm a broken record on this point, I shall stress again the importance of editing. First drafts are messy, and clarity cannot co-exist with messiness. If there's a wiggling doubt that you've made things clear enough, do another round of edits!

CHAPTER 67
Let Your Voice Find YOU

There are countless books, articles, and courses about how to find your voice as a writer. And a robust population of online gurus are eager to help you search, usually for a fee.

But here's the truth: It's all foolishness. You don't find your voice, it finds you.

You write. And write. And write. You focus on the nuts and bolts of the process—words, grammar, and structure. Eventually, you start to notice certain words and phrases that just feel right. They come to you effortlessly and when you look at them on the page, they feel like *you*. That's your voice.

It's not something you can consciously create or borrow from another writer. But you can nurture your voice:

- Find time to write for pleasure instead of for a pay cheque, because your voice needs to play and run free.

- Try different forms of writing, like poetry and songwriting, so your voice can stretch and explore creative challenges.

- When editing, leave your voice intact, if possible. Don't axe those words and phrases that feel right unless it's 100% necessary.

With encouragement, your voice will grow stronger, more reliable, and more flexible.

Over time, you'll become able to mould your voice to match the topic and style of content you're writing. For example, the fun side of your voice may come out to play in an upbeat blog post but remain subdued if you're writing a technical paper. This is brilliant! It's exactly what you want your voice to do.

The best advice I can offer is to be patient. Don't stress yourself out trying to find your voice. Let it come to you. And once it appears, take good care of it. Because a clear, strong, adaptable voice is a writer's best friend.

CHAPTER 68
Save Your Scraps

Scenario: You find a brilliant quote to use as the opener for an article. It works well. Then, midway through the edit process, you come up with a creative anecdote that works better.

So, what do you do with that quote?

Please don't tell me you delete it!

Pearls of wisdom are precious, and the human memory is a sieve, not a vault. So, if there's even a slim chance of using that quote in the future, you should save it.

I have a folder titled "Scraps". Inside it are files filled with things like:

- Quotes

- Images

- Facts and figures related to various topics (with links to sources)

- Ideas for short posts, long-form articles, and guides

- Testimonials and kind words from clients and collaborators

- G-rated knock-knock jokes, one-liners, and wordplays

- Cool words and phrases I've bumped into online that deserve to end up in something at some point. *I'm currently keen to use "oomph", "bamboozled", and "whimsical" because they have such delicious sounds to them. Don't you agree?*

- Personal anecdotes that didn't make the final cut for a particular bit of writing but are still super amusing

- Abandoned rough drafts

Sometimes, randomly exploring my scrap collection sparks my creativity. Other times, it's more of a resource centre where I go for fast fixes and ways to add *oomph* to whatever I'm working on.

Ta-dah! Pulled that OOMPH out of my "cool words and phrases" file.

CHAPTER 69
Reduce. Re-use. Recycle

I've honed my time management skills in the trenches, juggling the infinite responsibilities of motherhood and work life over decades. And my strongest piece of advice is to **focus on maximizing the output from each effort.**

For example, give me a chicken and some vegetables and I'll give you at least three meals. On the first night, I'll produce a full roast chicken dinner. On the second night, I'll make soup and sandwiches. And on the third night, I'll reinvent the leftovers as a tasty casserole.

Waste not, want not. That's my motto.

Writing long-form content is hard. It takes considerable time and effort, so you want to make as many meals out of each piece as you can. The options may differ, depending on the length, topic, and audience, but in general, you can re-purpose a single piece of writing in three ways: reduce, re-use, and/or recycle.

Reduce options are about identifying elements within an in-depth piece of writing that have stand-alone potential. For example:

- Quotes, facts, and figures can become social media posts.

- Excerpts may work as shorter length blog posts.

- Sub-sections of interest to the business crowd might become LinkedIn articles.

Re-use options are about opening your mind and considering multiple purposes for one piece of content. For example, an in-depth white paper could become a signup incentive on a landing page or even a succinct e-book.

Recycling is about presenting your content in new formats. That same white paper might be formatted as a slide show, video, or e-learning course.

I start by pondering the reduce options because they're usually low effort. Then, when the original piece has aged a bit, I look at ways to re-use and recycle.

Ultimately, the goal is to maximize the value of your efforts. Pick every bit of chicken off the bones!

CHAPTER 70
Be Evergreen Whenever Possible

"You mustn't rely on flowers to make your garden attractive. A good bone structure must come first, with an intelligent use of evergreen plants so that the garden is always clothed, no matter what time of year."

Margery Fish, English Gardener and Gardening Writer

Wondering what an English gardening expert has to do with content writing?

Well, like writing, gardening is hard work. Flowers are beautiful, but short-lived. You're constantly planting and pruning. It's exhausting.

So, Margery Fish popularized the concept of the informal English country garden. In Margery's vision, evergreen plants were added to the mix because they stay lush and lovely throughout the seasons, without ongoing effort.

Current happenings and trends are like flowers. They capture attention when they first bloom, but they quickly fade away. If you're developing a collection of content to build authority, like a professional blog, writing exclusively about hot-button issues and events can be exhausting. Timely content loses steam quickly, so to keep people coming to the blog, you must perpetually create more and more posts.

See the problem?

As Margery would say... you need to plant some evergreens!

Evergreen content is just like those evergreen plants. It requires effort to get it into the mix, but once it has taken root, the maintenance needs are low—and the life expectancy is spectacular.

Evergreen content is the stuff people are *constantly* looking for. It includes things like:

- "How-to" articles

- Tips and tricks on general subjects, like motivation, productivity, and success

- Answers to frequently asked questions

- Checklists and templates

- Personal stories

- Information about historical events and people

While these topics may not go viral or produce immediate fame and fortune, they consistently attract readers. So, over time, they often perform better than time-sensitive fare. And they thrive with only an occasional review and refresh.

The most challenging part of creating evergreen content is that it's almost impossible to write something unique. That's simply the nature of the beast. No subject can be simultaneously timeless and new.

So, how do you write evergreen content that stands out and shines?

One option is to present a fresh perspective on a timeless topic. You might be able to approach things from a new angle or dive deep into a less explored aspect of the subject.

Another option is to aim for the highest possible quality level. Instead of trying to avoid writing about the same thing, charge into the fray with confidence. Have faith in your ability to make magic with your words. *All music is made from 12 basic notes, my friend. Some folks just play with them better.*

Creating evergreen content is a fantastic way to up your writing game, because it's less reliant on the latest facts and figures. When you don't have to spend as much time and effort gathering data, you can focus more on voice, tone, and style.

Ultimately, you probably want or need both timely and evergreen content on any professional website. The key is to be aware of the big picture and not fall into the habit of only planting flowers. Be sure to add evergreens!

How to Care for Evergreen Content

Like evergreen plants, your evergreen content may require seasonal pruning to continue looking its best:

- Change the featured image now and then

- Add quotes

- Update internal links to connect with newer, more timely content

- Add external links to authority websites

CHAPTER 71
Create Pillar Pages and Topic Clusters

The internet is polluted with content. Deep, vast pools of words cover every conceivable topic from every imaginable angle.

Search engines like Google are tasked with helping people find the best match for what they're looking for. But even after high-tech algorithms weed out the spammy content, the thin content, and the badly written content, there are still a wild number of options.

So, the Google Gods look at what's left and ask themselves, "Who's got the most authority?" That's where pillar pages and topic clusters come into play.

A **pillar page** is a deep dive into a topic that's right up your alley. It's comprehensive and super-informative, and it impresses readers with your brilliance and your expertise. It's the star of the show.

Like most celebrities, it has an entourage, a.k.a. the **topic cluster.** That's a collection of enthusiastic, hard-working articles that support your pillar page and engage readers with related content. Each member of the cluster gives shoutouts to the star (links to that pillar post). And they may also include links to each other, because they're a collaborative little gang!

Together, your pillar page and its growing circle of friends, convince both readers and the Google Gods that you're the bomb.

So, what should a pillar page look like?

It's the star, baby, and stars sparkle! While there are no hard and fast rules:

- A pillar page is usually long (2,000+ words). It's so long that it may have a table of contents, or at least a bunch of headings and sub-headings.

- The title announces its authority, with words like "Complete Guide" or "Ultimate Guide", or some other impressive adjective tacked onto the word "guide". *Pillar pages aren't the place for modesty.*

- The content is premium quality, comprehensive, and quotable.

Pillar pages merit—and require—lots of hard work. And you polish them like a red convertible. That said, it's important NOT to cover every aspect of the topic when writing a pillar page. *If it answers every question and solves every problem by itself, there's no reason for an entourage.*

Remember the Google Gods! They're not as attracted to one perfect piece of content as they are to a collection of pieces. It's that whole authority building thing.

You want your pillar page to be smart and showcase your brilliance, but don't elaborate on every insight. Leave some fodder for the cluster of related posts you haven't written yet.

CHAPTER 72
Don't Fear the Technical Stuff

"Continuous learning is the minimum requirement for success in any field."

Brian Tracey, Motivational Speaker and Author

Writing content may be your forte, but the internet is where your magical words live. And if you want them to thrive, you need to learn the lay of the land.

I describe myself as a "creative", not a "techie", but I've taken the time to learn how to use programs and apps that support my creative processes. I regularly peruse authority websites to stay up to date on search engine optimization trends. And I put in the work required to build engagement on social media platforms.

Is this the most fun part of my work? Definitely not!

Does it come easily to me? No again.

In fact, I frequently curse in frustration when trying to pretty things up for a website, and I would rather have a root canal than spend a morning hunting for backlinks. But these things are part of the deal.

Think of the technical elements as Brussels sprouts. Probably not the highlight of your meal, but nutritious and edible. Over time, you may even develop a taste for them.

I've come to enjoy making images on Canva, and I have lovely conversations on Twitter.

The secret is to lead with curiosity instead of trepidation. **Focus on the fun of learning new things.**

I set aside a morning every week for education. Sometimes, I use those hours to attend a webinar or take an online course. Other times, I just peruse the internet looking for cool new ways to create and promote content.

I also recommend booking time with experts. This is less expensive than you might imagine, and hugely productive. You can gain a wild amount of knowledge from spending just one hour with someone brilliant!

Tech stuff may never be your thing, but it will always play an integral role in the success of your content, and it's nothing to fear. *So, eat your Brussels sprouts.*

CHAPTER 73
Don't Be Prickly

"Criticism is something we can avoid easily by saying nothing, doing nothing, and being nothing."

Aristotle, Greek Philosopher

If you can't stand criticism of your writing, stick to journaling. I keep tons of journals and I love scribbling down my thoughts. It's both creative and cathartic, but it's not the same as writing for an audience.

So long as you are both the writer and the reader, you're in a bubble. No one takes offence at what you say or how you say it. But the moment you put words in front of an audience, you open yourself up to criticism. That's just the nature of the beast.

For the most part, criticism is a positive thing. You want someone to point out misspelled words so you can fix them. And if you've explained something poorly or said something that could be taken the wrong way, you want to be told!

In fact, you should invite this type of criticism. Have a few trusted people read your content before you hit publish. Test readers can tell you what's working and what isn't, and a reliable editor can help you polish your work until it sparkles.

FYI: Your mother may not be the best choice as either a test reader or an editor. Same goes for lovers, children, and people who owe you money.

Whether it's invited or uninvited, don't get prickly if someone suggests a tweak or offers up a thought you disagree with. Instead, examine your content from their perspective.

If you see their point, do the necessary edits and thank them for their opinion. If you don't see their point, do nothing, but still thank them for their opinion.

And if they're a client who is paying for your magical words, suck it up and make whatever changes are required. It's their content, not yours. Be a professional.

CHAPTER 74
Don't Cling to Old Work

Truth bomb: It's damn near impossible to produce brilliant work every time. And even the most spectacular content may eventually lose relevance.

For example, let's say you've been writing a blog post or a LinkedIn article every month for two years. That means you've got a collection of 24 pieces on that website or platform. *Congrats.*

But even if each one is beautifully written, I bet some are more popular than others, and a few are just taking up space.

You may also have evolved over those two years. Maybe you've pivoted a bit in terms of what you do, how you do it, and what you want to be known for. Or maybe you've found a niche. Either way, it's possible that some things don't fit your brand as well as they used to.

Over time, if you don't sort through things, the less purposeful stuff can accumulate and take over, like junk in an attic. So, at least once a year, it's important to do a holistic, objective review of *everything* on a website.

Often, older content can be refreshed with minimal effort. New images, new quotes, and updated headlines are just a few ways to blow the dust off and polish things up. But not everything is worthy of the effort.

When deciding what to save and what to toss, ask yourself: **Is anybody reading this?**

If you haven't learned how to track page traffic and engagement rates with tools like Google Analytics, figure it out! Measuring how well your work is performing is an integral part of being a content writer.

If a fair number of people are still reading a piece of content, try to save it. Organic traffic is lightening in a bottle. NEVER throw it out. But, if no one is visiting that page, ask yourself: **Is this topic still important and valuable to the readers I most want to attract?**

Sometimes, a subject simply loses relevance and it's time to say good-bye. But if the subject itself is still popular, you need to ponder one more question: **Will updating this be faster and easier than writing a whole new piece on this topic?**

A minor renovation may reinvigorate the traffic flow. For instance, something as simple as updating facts and figures could make an old article new again. That said, if the content is thin and doesn't meet your current quality standards, it may make more sense to say good-bye. Sometimes, starting from scratch is easier.

It's hard to let go, but housekeeping is a normal part of life. Everything is not equally special. To keep a website attractive and functional, some items simply must go.

Don't cling to old work. As my grandmother would say, "Get on with it. Clean up your crap."

Note: For those of you who freelance and write content for brands, it's worth mentioning that many organizations suffer from the plight of messy blogs and websites. Some of them will happily pay a content expert (*like you!*) to audit their existing posts and pages, and tidy things up.

CHAPTER 75
Do Other Stuff

**"A busy calendar and a busy mind will destroy
your ability to do great things in this world."**

Naval Ravikant, Entrepreneur and Investor

Writing is a skill, and like all skills, it improves with practice.
So, it stands to reason that you should write every day. Read
books on writing. Listen to podcasts. Take courses.

But beware of the rabbit hole.

Don't spend more time writing and thinking about writing
than you do living. Because life is what fuels creativity and
innovation. Schedule lots of writing time but make sure your
schedule includes hard stops. And leave enough open time on
your calendar to do other stuff.

Hang out with people. Expose yourself to different opinions.
Love. Argue. Kiss and make up. Get outside and have an
adventure. Stay inside and watch old movies. Learn how to
make sushi. *(FYI: It's harder than it looks.)*

Be curious about things that are happening in the world.

Don't think of downtime as something separate from your writing life. Instead, recognize it as an integral part of the creative process. You need to rest, connect with other humans, and do interesting things.

Honing your writing skills and communicating with your words is important. But having something interesting to say is priceless.

CHAPTER 76
Conquer Imposter Syndrome

**"I am not a writer. I've been fooling
myself and other people."**

John Steinbeck, Pulitzer Prize Winner

Let me make one thing perfectly clear. You ARE a writer.

The definition of a writer is "someone who writes." So, long as
you are managing to put words on a page, you're a writer. And
that nagging feeling that you're not a "real" writer, the way
other people are, is just silliness. It's all in your head.

That said, it's still a tough feeling, and I can relate because I
sometimes feel it myself. Not constantly, but more often than
you might think, given that I've been writing professionally
for decades.

I think of Imposter Syndrome as a chronic, yet treatable
condition. Here are a few things I recommend that may help
you manage the symptoms and avoid flare ups:

- **Keep a tangible reminder of your accomplishments.**

  My accomplishments live in a pickle jar. *Yes, you read
  that correctly.*

198

At the beginning of each new year, I place a sweet little pickle jar on the corner of my desk. Each time I complete a writing project for myself or for a client, I commemorate the moment using a colourful Post-it. I write the date and a few descriptive words on a little square and stick it in the jar.

As the months pass, my pickle jar becomes a cheery cornucopia of bright blues, yellows, oranges, and pinks. *I don't use the lime green Post-its because they're gross.* On the last workday of the year, I ceremoniously read each slip of paper and give myself a robust dose of self-appreciation. It's a lovely feeling.

If a pickle jar filled with Post-its doesn't match your style, feel free to customize the concept. *And I guess you can use the lime green Post-its if they don't repulse you.* The point is to acknowledge and honour your work, so the medium is less important than the message!

- **Learn how to embrace a compliment**

This is hard for lots of writers, me included. But it's a skill worth practising because it's important to be able to LISTEN and HEAR the good stuff.

When someone compliments your writing, resist the urge to say something like "It was no big deal" or "It could have been better". Instead, smile and say thank you. Consciously take a moment to let their kind words sink in and warm your soul.

- **Avoid comparison**

  Before you start writing, it may be smart to read what other folks have already published on the subject. But after you've finished writing, you need to let your work stand alone and stop measuring it against other pieces. As C.S. Lewis, author of *The Chronicles of Narnia*, once said, "Comparison is the thief of joy."

- **Keep writing**

  Doubt breeds in stillness. The longer I go without writing, the more I doubt myself and my abilities. But once I start clicking away on the keyboard, my brain begins to focus on ideas and words and stops paying attention to my annoying inner critic. Perseverance is victory.

The good news about Imposter Syndrome is that it's associated with being outside your comfort zone. So, congratulate yourself for having the courage to try new things and pursue your ambitions. Most of the best things in life happen just outside that comfort zone, so keep pushing yourself.

You've got this!

THANK YOU FOR READING

Thank you for reading my book. Or skimming it. Or popping into a chapter or two that struck your fancy. *No judgment. I'm just happy you're here.*

I hope you picked up a few tips and tricks to help you play with words, but most of all, I hope you caught the positivity I was trying to send your way. **You have everything it takes to be a fantastic content writer, so keep at it. Enjoy your work and take pride in your accomplishments.**

If you liked my book, I would greatly appreciate a positive review on Amazon, or Goodreads, or wherever you found it. And if you want to stay in touch, please follow me on Twitter or Instagram. Just hunt down @kimscaravelli and hit FOLLOW.

Kim

ABOUT THE AUTHOR

Kim Scaravelli, B.A., B.Ed., is an award-winning content strategist and writer with 20+ years of experience. She is the Founder and CEO of Trust Communications, an online content and communications company with clients across Canada, the United States, and Europe. Her writing appears on more than 400 corporate and non-profit websites.

Kim is also a keynote speaker, mom, and butler to several demanding pets. And she deeply enjoys being a writer.

Made in the USA
Middletown, DE
22 July 2022

69885446R00124